MANHOOD
101

101 Principles for Becoming a Better Man

Eric M. Watterson

MANHOOD 101:
101 Principles for Becoming a Better Man

CENTRY™ Curriculum
© 2017 All rights reserved.
ISBN: 978-1-533-50085-4
Visit Us Online At: CENTRY.me

Printed in the United States of America. All rights reserved. No part of this book may be reproduced in whole or in part in any form without the express written consent of the publisher.

Why This Book & How It Will Help?

One day I watched a young teen couple walk through a parking lot after taking pictures for what seemed to be the prom. As they walked side by side, the girl juggled her purse and two other bags, while struggling to walk in a pair of high heels that she obviously wasn't used to. As she struggled, her date walked beside her with both hands in his pockets never offering to help. After I got over being mad at him for his insensitivity, the thought came to me, "Does he know how to be sensitive and treat a young woman?" "Can I really be upset with this young man for not displaying honor if no man has showed him what honor is?"

Every male is born with an innate desire to lead. However, the ability to lead must be taught and developed; it's not automatic. The principles that were taught and practiced by men of character years ago are being loss today. We need to instill the standards and principles that develop boys into quality men that women love to be in relationship with and create men that help children feel loved, protected and cared for. The purpose of this book is to help males reconnect to the standards and principles of quality manhood in a simple and easy to read format.

My sincere desire is that every man that truly wants to display a lifestyle of quality manhood to do just that. This book is intended to help with that goal by explaining 101 simple and practical principles of manhood so that they can be discussed, practiced and applied in every male's life.

To Your Success,

Eric M. Watterson

TABLE OF CONTENTS

INTRODUCTION _____ 9
I UNDERSTANDING _____ 13
  #01 Men Create Men _____ 15
  #02 Every Male Isn't A Man _____ 17
  #03 Always Willing To Learn _____ 19
  #04 Manhood Is A Choice _____ 21
II STANDARDS _____ 23
  #05 Standards Are Taught _____ 25
  #06 Find Worthy Teachers _____ 27
  #07 Avoid Low Standards _____ 29
  #08 Pursue High Standards _____ 31
  #09 It's What You Do; Not You Know _____ 33
III RESPONSIBILITY _____ 35
  #10 Master Critical Thinking _____ 37
  #11 Blame Is Immature _____ 39
  #12 Accept Responsibility For Others _____ 41
  #13 Being Wrong, Isn't Wrong _____ 43
  #14 Seek Correction, Not Praise _____ 45
  #15 Someone's Always Watching _____ 47
  #16 Be Worth Following _____ 49
IV MOTIVES _____ 51
  #17 Actions Have A Source _____ 53
  #18 Words Have A Source _____ 55
  #19 Pride Proceeds A Fall _____ 57
  #20 Know Who's Most Important _____ 59
  #21 Be Happy With You _____ 61
V INTEGRITY _____ 63
  #22 The Integrity Of Words _____ 65
  #23 Integrity In Relationships _____ 67
  #24 Integrity In Commitments _____ 69
  #25 Integrity In Decisions _____ 71
  #26 Integrity For Others _____ 73
  #27 An Integrity Mindset _____ 75

VI HONOR — 77
- #28 Honor Authority — 79
- #29 Highly Honor Women — 81
- #30 Give Honor From Honor — 83
- #31 Receive Honor From Honor — 85

VII DECISIONS — 87
- #32 Evaluate Past Decisions — 89
- #33 Stop, Think & Decide — 91
- #34 Benefit Your Family — 93
- #35 Learn From Bad Decisions — 95
- #36 Get Help With Your Decisions — 97

VIII SEPARATION — 99
- #37 Avoid The Crowd Mentality — 101
- #38 Don't Be A Bystander — 103
- #39 Adjust Friendships — 105
- #40 Avoid Peer Pressure — 107
- #41 Avoid Manipulation — 109
- #42 Recognize Distractions — 111
- #43 The Strength Of Walking Alone — 113

IX HURTS — 115
- #44 Understand Your Hurt — 117
- #45 Real Men Do Get Hurt — 119
- #46 Learn From Your Hurts — 121
- #47 Accept Hurt To Heal — 123
- #48 Forgiving Hurts Benefits You — 125

X ADJUSTMENTS — 127
- #49 Good Intentions & Good Actions — 129
- #50 Ignorance Will Cost You — 131
- #51 Change Your Thoughts & Actions — 133
- #52 Learn to Listen — 135
- #53 The Strength To Change — 137
- #54 The Strength To Repent — 139
- #55 Growth Requires Consistency — 141
- #56 Greatness By Helping Others — 143

XI MISTAKES — 145

#57 Bad Results, Aren't Always Bad _____ 147
#58 Try, Fail, Learn & Try Again _____ 149
#59 Ask, What Have I Learned? _____ 151
#60 Learn From Others _____ 153

XII LOVE _____ 155
#61 A Man's Unconditional Love _____ 157
#62 Lead With Your Love _____ 159
#63 Love For Yourself _____ 161
#64 Love For God _____ 163
#65 Real Love, Not Temporary Lust _____ 165

XIII WOMEN _____ 167
#66 Recognize Her Worth & Purpose _____ 169
#67 Mistreating Her, Impacts You _____ 171
#68 Your Strength Benefits Her _____ 173
#69 Lead Her And Please Her _____ 175
#70 Sex Isn't Just Physical _____ 177
#71 PORN Destroys Lives & Love _____ 179

XIV APPLICATION _____ 181
#72 Let Your Actions Speak _____ 183
#73 Judge Yourself Consistently _____ 185
#74 Judge Yourself Honestly _____ 187
#75 Practice Towards Perfection _____ 189
#76 Let It Out & Talk _____ 191
#77 Expect What You've Given _____ 193
#78 Understand And Control _____ 195

XV LEADERSHIP _____ 197
#79 Share Your Mistakes _____ 199
#80 See Yourself In Others _____ 201
#81 Understand, Not Condemn _____ 203
#82 Share The Good _____ 205

XVI GROWTH _____ 207
#83 Set Your Own Trend _____ 209
#84 Replace Negative Thoughts _____ 211
#85 Be Strong Enough To Get Help _____ 213
#86 Use The Strength Of Numbers _____ 215

#87 Live Positive Without Apology ___ 217
XVII DISPLAY ___ 219
  #88 Love Strong; Love Hard ___ 221
  #89 Appreciate & Listen To Women ___ 223
  #90 A Quality Man's Friend ___ 225
  #91 One In A Million ___ 227
XVIII LIFESTYLE ___ 229
  #92 Understand Purpose ___ 231
  #93 Find Your Core Brothers ___ 233
  #94 Be Selfless, Not Selfish ___ 235
  #95 Focus On The Fruit ___ 237
  #96 It's About Others ___ 239
  #97 Acknowledge Your Creator ___ 241
XIX GUARD ___ 243
  #98 Guard Your Gates ___ 245
  #99 Guard Your Brother ___ 247
  #100 Guard Your Words ___ 249
  #101 Guard Your Decision ___ 251
CLOSING TOGETHER ___ 253
BIBLIOGRAPHY ___ 255
OTHER BOOKS ___ 257
FOLLOW US ___ 259
MORE INFORMATION ___ 261

INTRODUCTION

The one hundred and one principles that are described here are meant to help every male become a man that expresses true manhood in his everyday life. Not based on age, but on his lifestyle that positively impacts women, children, families, communities and generations to come. It's time for men to truly be men and provide our young males with quality examples to follow. The concepts here may take a mindset shift for some; however, it's possible for the males who want to be strong; who want to serve; who want to live in honor; and, who want to protect our women, our children, our families and our world as true expressions of manhood.

The standards, beliefs, principles and conditions that created a thriving and successful society years ago have not changed or grown old fashion. So, what we will discuss is not new. However, a solid decision is needed if they are to become real in a man's life.

Each section is also broken into smaller sections for a quick read. If the principles are completely foreign to you, read them over a couple of times to completely understand them. Finally, each section has a summary Manhood Statement that we suggest that you read out loud. We believe this is vitally important because it's by our words we accept or reject thoughts and concepts. So, if you really believe and want to possess what each section discusses, say it out loud and begin the process of making it a reality. We really want to see change in your life and this world. So, it's by the words we hear, the words we believe, and the words we say that will help that become a reality.

I've had the honor of interacting with males, young and old, from different cultures, backgrounds, nationalities, upbringings and beliefs and there seems to be a lasting principle that's consistent with them all. This principle appears to be a foundational truth that each male will have to accept, operate in and will be held accountable to, this principle is the principle of choice.

We all have the ability to choose right or wrong, good or bad, light or darkness. Its by the choice that each of us make as males that determines the outcome of our lives, relationships, marriages, children and the overall impact we have on the world around us. Unfortunately, some males have not been shown "how" to choose what's right and are only being presented with what's wrong. How can a young man be expected to choose the light, if only the dark is being presented to him?

The 101 Principles of Manhood located within this book are designed to help males choose those things that have a positive impact on himself and those around him. If a male has not had a positive example in his life to help him choose, we want this book to help give him some of the foundational principles needed to become a man of greatness.

The women, children and youth of our society and world desperately need strong and positive men that will serve, honor and protect them. So, if you are reading this book, the world needs you. Thanks so much for taking this journey with us!

Ok, let's get started.

"When I was a child, I talked like a child, I thought like a child, I reasoned like a child; now that I have become a man, I am done with childish ways and have put them aside."
~ 1 Corinthians 13:11 AMP

* * *

"Boys will be boys, and so will a lot of middle-aged men."
~ Kin Hubbard

I
UNDERSTANDING

"Understanding Manhood"

understand [uhn-der-stand] verb - to perceive the meaning of; grasp the idea of; comprehend: \apprehend clearly the character, nature, or subtleties of: to assign a meaning to; interpret: to grasp the significance, implications, or importance of: to regard as firmly communicated;

Just because a male is tall, strong and has learned a few things, doesn't mean that he's truly a man or that he understands what real manhood is. Manhood is defined as, *"the state or time of being a man or adult male person; male maturity; traditional manly qualities; maleness, as distinguished from femaleness."* For our goal, we will focus on, *"traditional manly qualities"*. There are certain things that women and children expect from a "real man". Things that help marriages thrive and families survive. These are the things that display true manhood.

"I hate the company of evildoers and will not sit with the wicked."
~ Psalm 26:5 AMP

* * *

"Trust men and they will be true to you; treat them greatly, and they will show themselves great."
~ Ralph Waldo Emerson

#01
Men Create Men

Most of us have probably heard the saying, "There's nothing new under the sun." This is also consistent with us as men. We learn to become who we are based largely on what we see around us. As humans we learn to desire primarily based on what is set before us or made available to us. If you walk into a waiting room and there's a large bowl of fruit on the coffee table, you will probably reach for one of them even if eating fruit was the furthest thing from your mind when you first walked into the room.

By seeing the fruit that was made available, you will most likely have a desire to have it. If there was no fruit on the table, you probably would not ask for it. So, what we *see* is most likely the source of the desires we have.

Manhood Statement
"I will become the Quality Man that other males can follow and learn how to become a good man from!"

"Train up a child in the way he should go; even when he is old he will not depart from it."
~ Proverbs 22:6 ESV

* * *

"Youth is a blunder; Manhood a struggle; Old Age a regret."
~ Benjamin Disraeli

#02
Every Male Isn't A Man

Contrary to popular opinion, just being a male doesn't automatically mean you're a man. There are a lot of things that males do that a man wouldn't do. A man should live by a set of standards that produce a life that is worth following, such as effectively helping others to become better. A lot of males today are having babies left and right and not raising them. A true man wouldn't do that.

A lot of males are taking on characteristics of pop stars and celebrities that don't help them at all in their daily lives; a true man knows better than that. A lot of males steal from others to benefit their own selfish needs. A man doesn't take from others, but instead lives a life that benefits those around him.

Manhood Statement
"I will purposely do what's necessary to become a man of true quality!"

"Even the wise could become wiser by listening to these proverbs. They will gain understanding and learn to solve difficult problems."
~ Proverbs 1:5 ERV

"A little learning is a dangerous thing but a lot of ignorance is just as bad."
~ Bob Edwards

#03
Always Willing To Learn

One of the first things to make sure you keep in mind is that you must "*not know*" to truly open your mind, body and spirit so that you "*can know*." If you are going to grow into a strong man, you must first understand that you are in need of growth. If you have grown into a good man what will it take to become a *better* man?

Great men are always learning new things, always growing in some way and always humble enough to climb no matter how high he has come. So, make a decision to "not know." Look for those who can help you become better and greater than you are right now. And let's face it; if you don't think you need to learn anything, you're actually a lot worse off than you think.

Manhood Statement
"I'm not too proud to keep learning what it means to be a true man and I will always look for ways to get better!"

"When I was a child, I spoke like a child, I thought like a child, I reasoned like a child. When I became a man, I gave up childish ways."
~ 1 Corinthians 13:11 ERV

"Men are like steel. When they lose their temper, they lose their worth."
~ Chuck Norris

#04
Manhood Is A Choice

So with that said, are you really ready for manhood and how bad do you want it? Are you really ready for the work it will take? Most women see men as big boys just looking to have fun and running from responsibility. The sad thing is that in many cases these women are correct. Will you be another tall boy or will you be one of the males who truly pursue manhood? Only you know the answer.

Growing into manhood doesn't just happen. It takes education, understanding, practice, work and commitment to develop from a boy to a man in your thinking, relationships and standards. If you truly choose manhood, you also by your choice, choose all the work and effort needed for you to become a man.

Manhood Statement
"I think and live like a quality man, instead of a childish boy in my mind and actions!"

"So that your trust (belief, reliance, support, and confidence) may be in the Lord, I have made known these things to you today, even to you."
~ Proverbs 22:19 AMP

* * *

"A superior man in dealing with the world is not for anything or against anything. He follows righteousness as the standard."
~ Confucius

II
STANDARDS

"The Standards Of Manhood"

standard [stan-derd] noun - something considered by an authority or by general consent as a basis of comparison; an approved model. an object that is regarded as the usual or most common size or form of its kind: a rule or principle that is used as a basis for judgment: an average or normal requirement, quality, quantity, level, grade, etc.: standards, those morals, ethics, habits, etc. established by authority, custom, or an individual as acceptable:

Standards are the qualities or principles that you govern your life by. A man's quality standards will lead him towards actions that are selfless, helpful and constructive to others; another man's inferior standards will lead him towards actions that are selfish, childish and destructive. It's our standards that help to create quality actions and lives. Without quality standards you won't have a quality life. A society of people who live void of quality standards are a society of people void of quality life.

"Thus says the Lord: Learn not the way of the [heathen] nations and be not dismayed at the signs of the heavens, though they are dismayed at them,"
~ Jeremiah 10:2 AMP

* * *

"Tell me and I forget, teach me and I may remember, involve me and I learn."
~ Benjamin Franklin

#05
Standards Are Taught

Sometimes we have no idea why we do what we do or where specific behaviors come from. We learn standards from somewhere; be it through our environment, families, leaders and friends. Although we are all taught standards from multiple sources, we must understand *how* we are taught.

We're all products of what we're exposed to. What you see and experience will have an effect on you. For example, if you are raised by a family of thieves that are constantly thinking of new ways to take and steal, odds are you will most likely become a thief. So, when it comes to becoming a man, whether or not you achieve manhood is strongly dependent, but not limited to, the types of men who are around you. Exposure to them will affect who you will become.

Manhood Statement
"I evaluate my standards to make sure they're helping me become a better man."

"Follow my example, just as I follow the example of Christ."
~ 1 Corinthians 11:1 ERV

* * *

"Two men look out through the same bars: One sees the mud and one the stars."
~ Frederick Langbridge

#06
Find Worthy Teachers

Take a good look at the males around you, and those who teach you manhood, and examine whether or not they're good teachers. Once again, a male isn't a man, and every male doesn't display manhood. So, examine the males around you and be honest about what they're teaching you. Only allow yourself to be taught by quality examples of manhood and you'll become a teacher to those with low standards.

Take the time and find examples of the type of man you want to be and learn from him. If you can't find one male example with all the qualities of true manhood, learn from him the positive and ignore the negative. Search for the principles that are worth following and be mature enough to ignore those principles that are not. If a male isn't leading you to manhood, don't follow him.

Manhood Statement
"I only follow quality males that display true manhood in their lives!"

"You who are ignorant, learn to be wise. You who are foolish, get some common sense."
~ Proverbs 8:5 ERV

* * *

"Use soft words and hard arguments."
~ English Proverb

#07
Avoid Low Standards

Standards are not measured the same. Low standards benefit very few people and should be judged by how many lives it impacts positively. The smaller the positive impact, the lower it is. For example, racism is a low standard because it limits how many people can be positively loved and honored based on differences. It causes division and limits our ability to benefit from the differences in others, while unity enhances interaction between people despite their differences.

So low standards only benefit one person and/or a certain group of people. Its results are temporary and creates separation without growth. A low standard can be considered selfish and mostly benefits the source of the standard first, and then others last, if at all.

Manhood Statement
"I avoid low standards that only benefit me and my own selfish needs or desires!"

"Wisdom stands at the top of the hill, by the road where the paths meet. You who are ignorant, learn to be wise. You who are foolish, get some common sense."
~ Proverbs 8:2, 5 ERV

* * *

"Heroes walk alone; while followers stay at home."
~ Eric M. Watterson

#08
Pursue High Standards

A "High Standard" is a standard or principle that benefits many people and not just the person who operates in it. High standards will positively affect yourself and others. They will also create opportunities for growth and positive communication for everyone that's involved. For example, the act of forgiveness is a high standard because it enhances relationships and opens the door to restoration, learning and growth.

Forgiveness is a high standard because it benefits the person that's being forgiven and the person that's giving forgiveness. So, both parties are benefited by the high standard of forgiveness. Avoid actions and beliefs that only benefit you and have no positive impact on others. Make it a point to pursue the high standards that not only benefit you, but others as well.

Manhood Statement
"I purposely display the type of high standards in my life that benefit others before they benefit myself!"

"Even children show what they are like by the things they do. You can see if their actions are pure and right."
~ Proverbs 20:11 ERV

* * *

"Act as if what you do makes a difference. It does."
~ William James

#09
It's What You Do; Not You Know

We all know those people who just seem to like to instruct others, but don't like to be instructed. It's easy to instruct a person on the "right" thing to do. However, it's not so easy to be the person that actually does the "*right*" thing on a consistent basis. Most of us *know* the right thing to do, but how many of us actually *do* the right thing that we know to do.

As men, we often say that we are "The Heads of Our Houses" and we expect others to follow us. But if we don't make decisions that benefit our wives, children and others, not just ourselves, are we really worth following? You don't deserve to lead just because you're a male. Just like a boy doesn't deserve to drive a car just because he has two hands and his feet can reach the peddles! Become a man that moves beyond "*knowing*" what's right to actually "*doing*" what's right.

Manhood Statement
"As a quality man I do the right thing, because it's the right thing to do!"

"If you become wise, it will be for your own good. If you are rude and show no respect, you are the one who will suffer."
~ Proverbs 9:12 ERV

* * *

"Freedom comes from taking responsibility; bondage comes from giving it away."
~ Henry Cloud

III
RESPONSIBILITY

"Responsibility In Manhood"

responsibility [ri-spon-suh-bil-i-tee] noun - the state or fact of being responsible, answerable, or accountable for something within one's power, control, or management. an instance of being responsible; a particular burden of obligation upon one who is responsible; a person or thing for which one is responsible: reliability or dependability

There's a responsibility that comes from being a man, that doesn't apply if you're just a male. Males act on what they want for themselves. A man acts on what is best for those around him. Males pursue what they want no matter who it may hurt. Men pursue what helps others no matter how it effects themselves.

If you want to operate in manhood you must understand the responsibility that's involved in being a strong quality man.

"I looked at this and thought about it. This is what I learned: a little sleep, a little rest, folding your arms, and taking a nap — these things will make you poor very quickly."
~ Proverbs 24:32-34 ERV

"The essence of the independent mind lies not in what it thinks, but in how it thinks."
~ Christopher Hitchens

#10
Master Critical Thinking

Critical thinking can be described as "the skill or ability to purposely judge the effect and outcome of an action that you're about to take, before you actually do it." It's the act of thinking about your actions before you do them. Critical thinking is evaluating your actions to determine whether or not the worst possible outcome is acceptable to you and those around you.

Critical thinking evaluates if what you're about to do, or say, is worth the possible effects or consequences that may happen as a result. It's the evaluation of whether or not "what could happen" is acceptable and worth the risk. As a quality man, if you apply critical thinking prior to every action you make, and every word you speak, you'll save yourself and the people that will be affected by them, a lot of drama and heartache.

Manhood Statement
"I evaluate my actions to make sure that every possible outcome is beneficial!"

"People ruin their lives with the foolish things they do, and then they blame the Lord for it."
~ Proverbs 19:3 ERV

* * *

"The blame game is already a lost game, so don't attempt dressing up to play it!"
~ Israelmore Ayivor

#11
Blame Is Immature

Quality men don't pass blame. They accept responsibility and the consequences that are the result of situations he's attached to. This can also include the things he didn't mean to happen and may not have even been around for. A strong man looks for where his part is in situations and does not try to remove himself from them.

So if you are consistently blaming others for the things that happen in your life, this practice will most likely ensure that at the very least two conditions always remain in your life: #1 – you will never grow beyond the issues and circumstances around you because your too childish to accept what you need to do to change them; #2 – you will remain a child because children would rather pass blame than accept it and grow up.

Manhood Statement
"Instead of looking for someone to blame, I accept my faults and look to get better!"

"Good people say things that help others, but the wicked die from a lack of understanding."
~ Proverbs 10:21 ERV

* * *

"Being a selfless man in a selfish world isn't easy; but so worth it."
~ Eric M. Watterson

#12
Accept Responsibility For Others

One thing every quality man will need to do is accept responsibility. However, a quality man that's operating in manhood is willing to accept responsibility for others as well. In business, the overall success of the company is based on the leadership. If there are employees or processes that don't further the company, it's important that the leader takes it upon himself to train, motivate or replace anything or anyone that may hinder the success of the company. This mindset is one that accepts responsibility for success and failure even when others are involved.

When it comes to your marriage, family career and life, you must be strong enough to accept responsibility for others and make decisions that will enhance positive growth and development without pointing fingers.

Manhood Statement
"I accept responsibility for others and show them help and support in any way I can!"

"It's roots might grow old in the ground and its stump die in the dirt, but with water, it will grow again. It will grow branches like a new plant."
~ Job 14:8-9 ERV

"Failures are finger posts on the road to achievement."
~ C. S. Lewis

#13
Being Wrong, Isn't Wrong

Maturity is required if you want to be strong enough to accept responsibility. A mature man accepts responsibility when he's wrong. When he does, he learns. When he learns, he becomes better. When he becomes better, he becomes stronger. Becoming stronger is always a good thing. If getting stronger is a good thing, then being wrong isn't a bad thing but a good one.

Change your mindset when it comes to being wrong. If you're ever going to grow into a strong quality man that expresses manhood, you must learn to embrace your mistakes and the times when you're wrong. So instead of trying to prove yourself right and stay the same, embrace the times when you're wrong and grow into an expression of manhood.

Manhood Statement
"I don't mind being wrong or accepting my faults; it makes me better!"

"The Lord corrects the one he loves, just as a father corrects a child he cares about."
~ Proverbs 3:12 ERV

* * *

"The roots of true achievement lie in the will to become the best that you can become."
~ Harold Taylor

#14
Seek Correction, Not Praise

Don't seek praise for who you are as a man, husband, or father. Seek to become better and appreciation will follow. A strong man doesn't need to be praised for doing what's right, he just does it. What a strong man actually seeks is the correction that makes him better. Seeking to become better will result in praise and appreciation that's not needed but earned. It's a different result that will last a whole lot longer.

Don't seek praise for who you are or for what you've done. Some of the things you do as a husband, father, son and quality man, quite frankly, are your reasonable service. So, do them as an act of responsibility and always be open to the correction that can make you better, and avoid the praise that may only keep you stranded.

Manhood Statement
"I don't look for praise, but I constantly accept the correction that'll help me to become a better man!"

"The wicked are always looking for ways to kill good people."
~ Psalms 37:32 ERV

* * *

"Live among men as if God beheld you; speak to God as if men were listening."
~ Seneca

#15
Someone's Always Watching

Day by day we encounter different people that we're always leaving an impression on. Whether you recognize it or not, there is always someone who's watching you. There is always someone who will be impacted by your actions and may repeat them whether they were good or bad. As a man, there's always some other young man somewhere that's watching how you treat women, children, parents, authorities and others.

A quality man must be mindful of how his life impacts others. He understands that how he responds to situations in public and behind closed doors, is always being watched and effects someone positively or negatively. So, live a life that displays quality manhood, and enhances the life of those that are watching you.

Manhood Statement
"Knowing I'm being watched, I strive to constantly help and benefit others by what they see in me!"

"I will follow your teachings forever and ever."
~ Psalms 119:44 ERV

***

"I wasn't planning to lead, I was standing in the back and then everyone turned around."
~Avery Hiebert

#16
Be Worth Following

We've talked about the fact that someone is always watching you, so is what they see worth following? A male worth following has a positive impact on the people around him because of how he thinks, what he says and how he treats others. On the other hand, a male that's not worth following has a negative impact on the life of the people around him and the people he comes in contact with.

If you follow someone that has a negative impact on others, you will become someone who has a negative impact on others. So, as you pursue manhood, don't allow disrespect or dishonor to cause you to have a negative impact on others. Instead, be the type of male that's worth following because your thoughts and actions enhance the lives of others and the world around you.

Manhood Statement
"As much as I can help it, I display a life that is worth following in the way I treat women, children and others!"

"Fools die because they refuse to follow wisdom. They are content to follow their foolish ways, and that will destroy them."
~ Proverbs 1:32 ERV

"It is not as much about who you used to be, as it is about who you choose to be."
~ Sanhita Baruah

IV
MOTIVES

"Understand Manhood Motives"

mo·tive [moh-tiv] noun - something that causes a person to act in a certain way, do a certain thing, etc.; the goal or object of a person's actions:

Motives are the driving force behind what we do. They're made up of our beliefs and thoughts that lead us to act in certain ways, believe certain things, and move in certain directions. We categorize motives in the following two ways; *selfish and selfless*. "Selfish" motives focus primarily on oneself, what you want and what benefits you. While "selfless" motives focus primarily on others, how you can assist them and benefit them in some way. So, it's important to understand the motive behind what you do to be able to judge if you're operating in true manhood.

"Be careful! When you do something good, don't do it in front of others so that they will see you. If you do that, you will have no reward from your Father in heaven."
~ Matthew 6:1 ERV

* * *

"Do you want to know who you are? Don't ask. Act! Action will delineate and define you."
~ Thomas Jefferson

#17
Actions Have A Source

To really understand why you do what you do, you'll need to first understand what drives you. Your actions could be based in how you were taught or what you believe about yourself and the world around you. How males treat our women is largely based in how we think and what we've been taught. How we treat others is largely determined by how others have treated us and how we interpret and respond to those actions.

Understanding that every action has a source will make you purposely trace the source of your own actions to your root thoughts, beliefs, history, fears, etc. that cause them. Understanding this is vital for us as males if we want to replace negative actions with positive ones.

Manhood Statement
"I will examine my actions to make sure their source is good and beneficial for myself and those around me!"

"His words about peace are as smooth as butter, but he has only war on his mind. His words are as slick as oil, but they cut like a knife."
~ Psalms 55:21 ERV

"That's what careless words do. They make people love you a little less."
~ Arundhati Roy

#18
Words Have A Source

The words we speak have a source. If your goal is to get someone to do something for you, your words may be filled with guilt or blame. However, if your goal is to help someone, then your words may be of support and concern. The words you speak come from the motive of your heart. For example, if you say, "I told you so.", your goal is to prove yourself right or to get credit for something. However, if you use the words, "You can do it.", your goal is to help support someone when they need it.

So be mindful of the source of the words you speak. Whether your words are intended to give or to get, be honest about the source of your words and change the motives of your heart to give and not to take and your words will change accordingly.

Manhood Statement
"My words are intended to help and support someone else, not to hurt them!"

"Pride is the first step toward destruction. Proud thoughts will lead you to defeat."
~ Proverbs 16:18 ERV

* * *

"I am not proud, but I am happy; and happiness blinds, I think, more than pride."
~ Alexandre Dumas

#19
Pride Proceeds A Fall

Pride can be viewed as an excessive and elevated view of one's self. Having a good self-image is vital and important, but when it moves you to view yourself higher than others and above correction, you set yourself up to fail. When you see yourself higher, better and greater than others, you limit your own ability to learn, grow and see yourself properly. This stance will lead you towards a cliff that no one can help you to avoid.

Once you are convinced of your own high self-worth, others cannot advise you of the truth because you're too prideful to hear them. Always, keep a humble and modest opinion of yourself so that you can always be advised by others if you're ever too close to a fall.

Manhood Statement
"I won't allow a prideful self-image to cause me to view myself greater or above others or their advice!"

"Live a life of love. Love others just as Christ loved us. He gave himself for us — a sweet-smelling offering and sacrifice to God."
~ Ephesians 5:2 ERV

"Every time you smile at a someone, it is an action of love, a gift to that person, a beautiful thing."
~ Mother Theresa

#20
Know Who's Most Important

It's important to be honest about how we think about others and who's most important in any given situation. If you're talking with your wife, is she more important than you? If so, her feelings, thoughts and opinions matter. This does not mean you agree, but if she's important, her words and feelings will also be important. If what she says and how she feels doesn't matter to you, then her place in your heart is low and must be honored if your relationship is to last.

A quality man understands that others are always more important than himself. He purposely loves, serves and helps others knowing that when he does, he'll be loved, served and helped as well.

Manhood Statement
"I always place others and their needs above myself so that I can always be in a position to serve and help!"

"He makes us happy. We trust his holy name."
~ Psalms 33:21 ERV

* * *

"Recommend to your children virtue; that alone can make them happy, not gold."
~ Ludwig van Beethoven

#21
Be Happy With You

We all have an internal voice that speaks to us, especially during our quiet times. It talks to us about who we are and what we desire. It's at these times we can truly judge how we feel about our lives and our decisions. If you're unhappy on the inside, it may be a clear sign that you should make some changes towards a new path.

Feelings of unhappiness are most likely a cry for a purpose that's not selfish or empty. It's this voice that people sometimes try and drown out with drugs, alcohol, sex and/or other addictions. All of which don't quiet the voice, just limits your ability to hear it. If you want to pursue happiness within yourself, find someone else that you can make happy. When we focus our attention on helping others, our service to them serves us.

Manhood Statement
"I'm happy with myself and create a happy life for my woman, children and others!"

"Good people are guided by their honesty, but crooks who lie and cheat will ruin themselves."
~ Proverbs 11:3 ERV

* * *

"To starve to death is a small thing, but to lose one's integrity is a great one."
~ Unknown Author

V
INTEGRITY

"The Integrity Of Manhood"

integrity [in-teg-ri-tee] noun - adherence to moral and ethical principles; soundness of moral character; honesty. the state of being whole, entire, or undiminished: to preserve the integrity of the empire. a sound, unimpaired, or perfect condition: the integrity of a ship's hull.

Integrity is an outward display and lifestyle of quality standards, principles and beliefs. It's how a strong quality man shows the people around him that his words, actions and lifestyle can be trusted. It's by a man's integrity that he displays to the world that he lives on a higher level of standards than other childish males. It's a man's integrity that will help him to consistently make quality decisions that benefit those that he loves no matter what temptations, situations and/or circumstances may try to challenge it.

"It is better to be poor and honest than to be a liar and a fool."
~ Proverbs 19:1 ERV

* * *

"Your word is the only thing you can give and keep at the same time."
~ Carlos Wallace

#22
The Integrity Of Words

Years ago, before contracts and lawyers became common place, agreements were made by a man's word and a handshake. In all fairness, there are times when you can't do what you said. At these times, a man of integrity "takes responsibility" for his words and explains "why" what he said will not happen. He then apologizes for it and reschedules if possible. A man of integrity will address his commitments, agreements and words when they fall short.

By doing this, he expresses the importance and integrity of his words and shows others he can be trusted when he speaks. So, make your words important to you and people will trust them. Make every effort to show the world the quality man you are by the quality words you speak.

Manhood Statement
"My words can be trusted and I make sure to follow through with all of my verbal agreements and commitments!"

"But Joseph refused. He said, 'My master trusts me with everything in his house. He has given me responsibility for everything here. I cannot sleep with his wife! That is wrong! It is a sin against God.'"
~ Genesis 39:8-9 ERV

* * *

"We have to recognize that there cannot be relationships unless there is commitment, unless there is loyalty, unless there is love, patience, persistence."
~ Cornel West

#23
Integrity In Relationships

What if we viewed our most valuable relationships and connections like contracts or agreements made with people? The more important the people, the more important the agreement. And these important agreements would be mutually beneficial for all parties involved. So, if you were to mistreat the person, you destroy the integrity of the contract and the trust that the person has given to you. Treat every relationship that you have as a valuable contract and place a high level of integrity upon yourself to honor it.

You must guard and protect the people you have relationship with from temptations and your own dishonorable and selfish actions. A man of integrity will be faithful to the relationships he has with his wife, children, family and his purpose and honors them no matter what.

Manhood Statement
"I purposely operate in integrity and show the people that I'm in relationship with that I can be trusted!"

"David's men were with us the whole time, and they never did anything wrong to us. They did not take anything from us."
~ 1 Samuel 25:15 ERV

* * *

"The only chains you should wear in life are the chains of commitment."
~ Shannon L. Alder

#24
Integrity In Commitments

The things we say are used by people to evaluate the quality of man we are. If you make a commitment that you don't follow through on, you show others that they shouldn't take your words seriously because you don't. If what you say can't be trusted it expresses that you, as a man can't be trusted.

When you purposely, display integrity in your commitments, you show those around you that you value your own words and who you are as a man. This helps them to expect integrity from you. When the actions you take line up with the words you say, you prove that your words are true. Our words create expectation in the hearts of others. The words you speak, only become true, when they agree with the actions you take.

Manhood Statement
"I am a man that can be trusted to honor and follow through with the words I speak and the commitments I make!"

"Keep your conscience clear. Then people will see the good way you live as followers of Christ, and those who say bad things about you will be ashamed of what they said."
~ 1 Peter 3:16 ERV

* * *

"Real integrity is doing the right thing, knowing that nobody's going to know whether you did it or not. "
~ Oprah Winfrey

#25
Integrity In Decisions

Every decision we make in life comes from within us. Who you are, what you think and the beliefs you have on the inside will determine the decisions you make. If you want to live a life that displays integrity, you must think and believe that integrity is an important way to live.

When you truly possess personal integrity, it will affect your decisions and how you interact with others. A man of integrity purposely evaluates the things that he does, and the words that he says, to make sure they agree with the standards that he has decided to live by. If the decision he's about to make passes his integrity checkpoint, it's something that he feels comfortable doing. However, if a decision does not line up with his life of integrity, it's not worth doing.

Manhood Statement
"I will purposely evaluate my decisions to make sure that my life constantly displays integrity to those around me!"

"Good people are guided by their honesty, but crooks who lie and cheat will ruin themselves."
~ Proverbs 11:3 ERV

* * *

"Integrity is telling myself the truth. And honesty is telling the truth to other people."
~ Spencer Johnson

#26
Integrity For Others

Men of integrity are mindful of others. The words they speak and the things they do show others that they matter and are valued. They understand that their actions effect someone in some way whether positive or negative. When a male purposely does something that has a negative effect on someone else, he shows his lack of honor and integrity for others.

Men of integrity don't do things that negatively impact others; they positively impact them. They don't make life harder for others; they look for ways to make things easier for others. They aren't selfish; they're selfless; They don't make promises and leave others hanging; they show others that they can be counted on. In essence, they are mindful of others which causes others to be mindful of them.

Manhood Statement
"I purposely live a life of integrity in how I treat and honor others!"

"Finally, brothers and sisters, keep your thoughts on whatever is right or deserves praise: things that are true, honorable, fair, pure, acceptable, or commendable."
~ Philippians 4:8 GW

"When we see men of a contrary character, we should turn inwards and examine ourselves."
~ Confucius

#27
An Integrity Mindset

True integrity begins as a quality mindset. Why? Because the situations and the circumstances in our lives will always change, however, the standard of integrity doesn't. If you're pursuing true unselfish manhood and want to show those around you that you can be relied upon, you will live and operate from a mindset of integrity no matter what. Either you do what you say you are going to do or you don't. Either people can count on you to fulfill your word or they can't. It's as simple as that.

Just because the situations we face in life will change, it doesn't mean we change with them. A man that operates from a mindset of integrity is trustworthy, consistent, honest, faithful, sincere and reliable. He doesn't impact the life of someone else negatively but looks for ways to touch others positively.

Manhood Statement
"I purposely develop a mindset of integrity that purposely looks to help and benefit someone else in some way!"

"Whoever can be trusted with small things can also be trusted with big things. Whoever is dishonest in little things will be dishonest in big things too."
~ Luke 16:10 ERV

"The difference between a moral man and a man of honor is that the latter regrets a discreditable act, even when it has worked and he has not been caught."
~ H. L. Mencken

VI
HONOR

"The Honor Of Manhood"

hon·or [on-er] noun - honesty, fairness, or integrity in one's beliefs and actions: a source of credit or distinction: high respect, as for worth, merit, or rank: such respect manifested:

Similar to integrity, honor is a way of life for true manhood. It's an internal condition that moves a man to show concern, respect and courtesy to others at all levels. To honor someone is to place them and their needs above your own. The actual level of honor that is given to each person may differ, but a man who truly operates in honor gives it to everyone that he comes in contact with. Whether it's a 5-star general in the armed forces or a young cashier at a burger stand, a man that operates in honor highly respects them both.

"Be willing to serve the people who have authority in this world. Do this for the Lord. Obey the king, the highest authority."
~ 1 Peter 2:13 ERV

"It is not titles that honour men, but men that honour titles."
~ Niccolò Machiavelli

#28
Honor Authority

Our parents, our teachers, our aunts and uncles, policeman, our employers and leaders have positions that give them authority over us that's meant to benefit us. When you don't honor those over you, you limit their ability to benefit your life. It will also negatively affect your life and how they can direct, train and cover you.

For example, if a boy disrespects his parents, he's limiting his ability to benefit from the love, protection and training they can give him. If we disrespect police officers, we limit the effectiveness of those officers to serve and protect us. As a man, you must understand the importance of honor and why you should make honoring authority part of your lifestyle. By doing so, you give them the right to help, instruct and serve you in any way they can.

Manhood Statement
"As a quality and wise male, I respect and honor authority so that I'm always in a position to benefit from them!"

"How hard it is to find the perfect wife. She is worth far more than jewels."
~ Proverbs 31:10 ERV

* * *

"What would men be without women? Scarce, sir...mighty scarce."
~ Mark Twain

#29
Highly Honor Women

One underestimated area of manhood is, the honor that we show women. Women are the ground by which life continues. Without women, men would come to an end. Women must be seen as gifts for any man who wants to operate in manhood. Men that don't honor women, dishonor themselves, especially in a marriage. A married man who abuses his wife abuses himself, because the covenant of marriage merges the male and female as one in body and soul.

Women are made for men to love, cherish and honor. The more a man honors a woman, the more he becomes a man of honor by practice and development. The more a man dishonors a woman, the less honor he will have inside of him and the less honor he will receive in his own life.

Manhood Statement
"I purposely love, honor and cherish the gift of women, despite the negative thoughts and beliefs of childish males!"

"Respect the Lord and be humble. Then you will have wealth, honor, and true life."
~ Proverbs 22:34 ERV

* * *

"I am not bound to win, but I am bound to be true. I am not bound to succeed, but I am bound to live up to what light I have."
~ Abraham Lincoln

#30
Give Honor From Honor

Have you ever heard the saying "stupid is, as stupid does."? In essence, what you do is an expression of who you are on the inside. If you abuse a woman or disrespect authority, it's actually a sign of your own immaturity. So, when you on purpose show honor and respect, you show the world that you have honor and respect within you; and not just for others, but for yourself as well.

Who you truly are on the inside cannot be hidden. If you find it hard to show honor to others, it's because there's a lack of honor within you. Examine your thoughts, feelings and beliefs to see what may be hindering you from possessing honor inside you. You can't give someone something you don't have, so make sure you have honor within you, so you have honor to give away.

Manhood Statement
"I purposely examine my thoughts, background and beliefs to make sure I have honor within me that I can give to others!"

"Do for other people everything you want them to do for you."
~ Luke 6:31 GW

* * *

"Honor is simply the morality of superior men."
~ H. L. Mencken

#31
Receive Honor From Honor

Honor seems to be lacking in our society, but it wasn't always this way. There have been so many examples of disrespect that it now seems normal to some people. So, we as men must, once again, take responsibility for this and show the honor of giving honor. We must live a life that shows when we honor someone else, someone else will honor us.

Keep in mind that, the honor that you receive is a result of the honor you give. When you honor someone, you will in return be honored. It's part of the cycle of what you do for others will be done unto you. If you want to be honored by someone, you must first give someone honor. Purposely be a man that gives honor and watch how much honor you will begin to receive in return; not by chance, but by choice!

Manhood Statement
"As a man of honor. I give honor to others knowing that I also deserve to be honored!"

"My son, it makes me happy when you make a wise decision."
~ Proverbs 23:15 ERV

"No great improvements in the lot of mankind are possible until a great change takes place in the fundamental constitution of their modes of thought."
~ John Stuart Mill

VII
DECISIONS

"Proper Manhood Decisions"

decision [dih-sizh-uh n] noun - The act or process of deciding; determination, as of a question or doubt, by making a judgement the act of or need for making up one's mind: something that is decided; resolution: the quality of being decided; firmness:

Some decisions we make are based on our selfish goals and desires and not on what's actually good or beneficial for us. At times we may blame people and situations for the things that happen, instead of understanding the impact that our decisions have on our lives. Positive outcomes in our lives are most often the result of the positive decisions we make; while negative outcomes are most likely the result of negative decisions.

To create positive outcomes in life, it's vital to develop a lifestyle of making positive decisions.

"Lord, you do what is right, and your decisions are fair."
~ Psalms 119:137 ERV

* * *

"Difficulties come when you don't pay attention to life's whisper. Life always whispers to you first, but if you ignore the whisper, sooner or later you'll get a scream."
~ Oprah Winfrey

#32
Evaluate Past Decisions

One way to see how good you are at making decisions is to judge the outcomes of your past decisions. Not to condemn yourself or to keep dwelling on past mistakes, but to help you understand if you need to change your decision making process.

Sometimes our intentions are positive, but our results are negative. If the outcome from a decision isn't what you hoped for, take the time to backtrack the steps that led you to that decision and learn from them, so you don't repeat them in the future. If you seem to be continually making the wrong decisions, you'll need to make some adjustments to help you make better ones. Taking the time to evaluate your past negative decisions, can help towards any adjustments that may be necessary to create the positive outcomes that you want to experience.

Manhood Statement
"I judge my past decisions to see if they're leading me towards the future that I want for me and my family!"

"Leave your old, foolish ways and live! Advance along the path of understanding."
~ Proverbs 9:6 ERV

***

"If anyone on the verge of action should judge himself according to the outcome, he would never begin."
~ Søren Kierkegaard

#33
Stop, Think & Decide

We've all had those moments in our lives where we've said to ourselves, "I shouldn't have done that." It's at these moments that we all wish we would have taken the time to stop, think and decide whether or not what we were about to do should have been really done in the first place. And consider how our actions may affect someone else.

To develop the ability to stop, think and decide you'll have to possess enough self-control to keep you from quick impulsive decisions. It's important to have a set of sound ideas and beliefs in place as the foundation of your actions to help guide and evaluate your decisions. Without this quality foundation, your decisions and actions may, most likely, end up impulsive, selfish and destructive.

Manhood Statement
"I make a decision to stop, think and decide concerning my decisions to make sure they're not impulsive and selfish!"

"He must be a good leader of his own family. This means that his children obey him with full respect."
~ 1 Timothy 3:4 ERV

* * *

"If someone were to harm my family or a friend or somebody I love; I would eat them. I might end up in jail for 500 years, but I would eat them."
~ Johnny Depp

#34
Benefit Your Family

A man of maturity doesn't think only about himself but thinks of others first, especially his family. So, when it comes to making decisions, he thinks of his family, his wife, his children and whoever else will be affected by his decisions. We all grow up being self-centered. We must purposely consider how our actions will affect our family and those around us. It's this quality that distinguishes a boy from a man.

A selfish and childish male doesn't consider how his actions will affect others and may never develop a lifestyle of manhood. If any boy wants to become a man, it's vital for him to make mature decisions that not only benefit himself, but also his family, his relationships and those around him.

Manhood Statement
"I don't make childish decisions that only benefit me, but that benefit my family and my relationships as well!"

"A decision that is fair makes good people happy, but it makes those who are evil very afraid."
~ Proverbs 21:15 ERV

* * *

"The only true wisdom is in knowing you know nothing."
~ Socrates

#35
Learn From Bad Decisions

The Wiktionary.org says, *"Hindsight is 20/20. (idiomatic) In hindsight things are obvious that were not obvious from the outset; one is able to evaluate past choices more clearly than at the time of the choice."* In essence, the things that we couldn't see clearly at the beginning are often glaringly obvious afterwards.

As we develop into manhood, it's important to evaluate and learn from the bad decisions we've made in the past. Childish males will consistently make bad decisions and blame everyone else but himself for their results. As we become better men, we learn from the bad decisions we've made in our past and make the adjustments needed to not repeat them in our future.

Manhood Statement
"I purposely evaluate and learn from the bad decisions that I've made in my past so I don't repeat them in my future!"

"You will make the right decision, because you can see the truth."
~ Psalms 17:2 ERV

* * *

"I always pass on good advice. It is the only thing to do with it. It is never of any use to oneself."
~ Oscar Wilde

#36
Get Help With Your Decisions

Ok...so let's be honest, if ya need help...ya need help! Every strong man that's living a life of manhood had to learn manhood from somewhere. It doesn't happen automatically and the guy walking next to you is most likely not the one to teach you. Why? Because he's probably just as ignorant as you are or he wouldn't be walking with you! So, look for someone wiser and smarter that's in the position you want to be in.

By finding a quality male to toss decisions and ideas around with, you open your life up to additional viewpoints and perspectives. Sometimes that's exactly what we as males need. Every quality man needs someone that he can trust to give him quality advice and insight on the specific areas of his life where he needs growth. So, make sure to get help with your decisions from a quality man that can help you make quality decisions.

Manhood Statement
"I find quality males in my life to help me make quality decisions!"

"When the king sits and judges people, he must look carefully to separate the evil from the good."
~ Proverbs 20:8 ERV

* * *

"There are some places in life where you can only go alone. Embrace the beauty of your solo journey."
~ Mandy Hale

VIII
SEPARATION

"Separation in Manhood"

sep·a·ra·tion [sep-uh-rey-shuhn] noun - an act or instance of separating or the state of being separated. a place, line, or point of parting. a gap, hole, rent, or the like. something that separates or divides.

As we have discussed, manhood is taught and learned. With that said, it can also be hindered and blocked. Both points lean heavily on your company, your influences, your leaders and your training. So, there will be times when you will need to separate yourself from situations and people if you are ever going to walk in manhood. Just like everything else that we discuss, this is by no means a complete list of what you should do, but a starting point to build upon. Just as every life is different, we all have different experiences. As you become a better man, learn when it's time to separate yourself to find your own path.

"A few good people are better than a large crowd of those who are evil."
~ Psalms 37:16 ERV

* * *

"Step out of the crowd of average people. Enter that game and change the values on the scoreboard."
~ Israelmore Ayivor

#37
Avoid The Crowd Mentality

Carefully judge the company and the crowd you hang with because it's easy to get caught up with the focus of a crowd, or what I call "The Crowd Mentality". When the crowd, decides to do a thing, either right or wrong, it's hard to separate from it. The crowd can be a group of friends, a gang, classmates, coworkers, the music you listen to or the popular trends you follow. Oftentimes if the crowd you are attached to decides to do a thing, it's much easier to just go along with it, than it is to break away.

There are many males in bad situations or even jail, because of their involvement with negative crowds. Their inability to break away from negative influences because they did not understand the "Crowd Mentality" has changed their life forever.

Manhood Statement
"I carefully decide the types of crowds I follow to make sure the crowd mentality doesn't negatively affect my life!"

"Some friends are fun to be with, but a true friend can be better than a brother."
~ Proverbs 18:24 ERV

* * *

"Heroes are ordinary people who make themselves extraordinary."
~ Gerard Way

#38
Don't Be A Bystander

The term "Bystander Effect" refers to the phenomenon where the greater the number of people present, the less likely a person is to help someone in distress. It also states that the probability of a person helping someone in need is directly related to the number of bystanders present. It displays how we have the ability to pass responsibility of taking action ourselves to someone else when we're in a group. This is why people tend to stand around and watch as part of a group instead of reacting as an individual when needed.

As a quality man, make a decision to act and assist everyone you can. Don't allow the crowd to determine your actions. Whenever a situation arises, don't get caught up by the bystander effect. Be a quality man of action that's ready to act and respond immediately and help when needed.

Manhood Statement
"I will not be just another bystander in the crowd but I will react when needed!"

"You can trust what your friend says, even when it hurts. But your enemies want to hurt you, even when they act nice."
~ Proverbs 27:6 ERV

* * *

"Confidence is knowing who you are and not changing it a bit because of someone's version of your reality is not their reality."
~ Shannon L. Alder

#39
Adjust Friendships

To achieve manhood, you have to be willing to adjust the friends around you who hinder that decision. If your goal is to develop into a better man, you'll need to separate yourself from boys, and start spending more time with quality men. If you don't have quality men around you to learn from, find them. Read a book, watch life documentaries, talk to some elders and/or join a nonprofit or community organization where quality men are available to learn from.

I'm not saying that you should kick negative friends completely to "the curb," because it may give the impression that you consider yourself better than them. Just make the needed adjustments to separate yourself from people and conversations that oppose your goal of becoming a better man.

Manhood Statement
"I adjust negative friendships and connections that can potentially hinder my development into manhood!"

"And now he can help those who are tempted. He is able to help because he himself suffered and was tempted."
~ Hebrews 2:18 ERV

* * *

"I'm not in this world to live up to your expectations and you're not in this world to live up to mine."
~ Bruce Lee

#40
Avoid Peer Pressure

Let's talk about peer pressure, but let's call it "temptation." When someone pressures you, they're actually trying to tempt you into doing something, either good or bad. The point to remember is that if you allow any temptation to continue in your life, you'll eventually yield to it, no matter what it is, it's just a matter of time.

Imagine if a rock is positioned underneath a constant drop of water. If given enough time, the drop of water will eventually eat through the rock, based on its consistency, not its strength. So, don't allow the wrong pressure or temptation to stay in your life, because if you do, it will eventually win! If you really want to not be moved from your quality standards, beliefs and decisions, don't allow negative peer pressure and temptations to remain in your life at all costs!

Manhood Statement
"I do not allow negative peer pressure or temptations to remain in my life!"

"This is what the woman said to tempt the young man, and her smooth words tricked him."
~ Proverbs 7:21 ERV

* * *

"When you know what a man wants you know who he is, and how to move him."
~ George R.R. Martin

#41
Avoid Manipulation

As humans, we all desire to feel acceptance, approval and know that we belong. There's nothing wrong with that. However, that desire can be manipulated and used incorrectly. We must make sure that this desire isn't used to manipulate our actions, and that we don't use it to manipulate others.

It's very important that we as men don't use manipulation against people to get what we want from them, like telling a woman to have sex with us if she loves us. A quality man doesn't use manipulation to influence and control women or others. A good man influences others by his love and quality standards. He doesn't use a person's desire for approval to accomplish his own selfish goals and needs.

Manhood Statement

"I will not use manipulation to accomplish my own desires and I will not allow myself to be manipulated by someone else!"

"Don't go to the right or to the left, and you will stay away from evil."
~ Proverbs 4:27 ERV

***

"Belief can be manipulated. Only knowledge is dangerous."
~ Frank Herbert

#42
Recognize Distractions

A quality man constantly judges his friends and connections to see if they are a benefit or a distraction to his life. For example, if a friend is cheating on his wife, is he a good friend? Probably not. Do you want his unfaithful mindset to affect you? Will his stories of infidelity create ideas in your own mind? Is the connection with him, worth you losing your wife, kids and life? In this case, he would be a distraction to your goal.

So, examine the people around you to see who are distractions and who are beneficial to your goal of manhood. If you need help to properly judge a friendship or situation, get additional insight from a quality person you trust. Be mature enough to value your goal of becoming a better man and recognize any relationships that are distractions and make the needed adjustments.

Manhood Statement
"I examine my friendships and connections to properly adjust any distractions!"

"You cleared a path for my feet so that I could walk without stumbling."
~ Psalms 18:36 ERV

***

"If you are never alone, you cannot know yourself."
~ Paulo Coelho

#43
The Strength Of Walking Alone

During our walk of manhood, there will be times that you'll need to walk alone. Our times of walking alone shouldn't be intended to remove people from our lives, but to help us judge and understand who we are, so we can become better men. Our alone times, give us a chance to reflect on what we've done, why we did it and who we want to be.

Walking alone gives us a chance to honestly evaluate what truly makes us happy and who we are on the inside without the need to please others. It's a great time to be honest with ourselves about what type of male we are today and make the needed adjustments towards being the type of man we want to be in the future. This type of honest evaluation, that we spend walking alone, is vital for a male to find that internal voice and strength that's needed to become a better man.

Manhood Statement
"I'm willing to walk alone and evaluate the man I am and the man I want to be!"

"Save me from those who want to hurt me, and I will obey your instructions."
~ Psalms 119:134 ERV

* * *

"Happiness is not the absence of problems, it's the ability to deal with them."
~ Steve Maraboli

IX
HURTS

"The Hurts Of Manhood"

hurt [hurt] verb - to cause bodily injury to; to damage or decrease the efficiency of (a material object) by striking, rough use, improper care, etc.: to effect adversely; harm: to cause mental pain to; offend or grieve: to feel or suffer bodily or mental pain or distress: to suffer want or need.

One of the worst things a man can do, is feel hurt, act as if it doesn't exist and hide behind other emotions like sarcasm or anger. We as men do feel hurt and have emotions. We may not express it the same way women do, but we really need to be honest about it. If we as men feel hurt and force it down inside of us without being honest and addressing it, it'll come up eventually. Unfortunately, when it does come up, it will probably be much more damaging to us and those around us because we believed the lie that said real men don't get hurt or cry.

"You have hurt me. You punished me and hurt me deeply."
~ Psalms 38:2 ERV

* * *

"Cry. Forgive. Learn. Move on. Let your tears water the seeds of your future happiness."
~ Steve Maraboli

#44
Understand Your Hurt

It'll be easier for males to accept hurt when we understand it. Feelings of hurt normally arise as a result of some expectation that wasn't met. This expectation can surround a situation, circumstance, desire, relationship, goal or anything that's important to us. When expectations go unmet, we can experience disappointment, sadness, pain, etc., all of which are part of life. When they happen, we should just accept and embrace our feelings, instead of acting as if they don't exist.

Things won't always go our way and we will get hurt. It's a fact of life. Don't expect or act as if you're above this fact because you're a male. Understand your hurts and learn from them. It's this process of learning and growth from hurts that'll set you apart from other immature males that hide behind their pain.

Manhood Statement
"I understand that getting hurt is a fact of life. I embrace and learn from it without acting as if it doesn't exist!"

"When I was safe and secure, I thought nothing could hurt me."
~ Psalms 30:6 ERV

* * *

"Every man has his secret sorrows which the world knows not; and often times we call a man cold when he is only sad."
~ Henry Wadsworth Longfellow

#45
Real Men Do Get Hurt

Contrary to popular "guy" opinion, it's ok to feel pain and to admit hurt. Only immature men say getting hurt is a sign of weakness. There's a great need for us as strong males to understand what it means to feel hurt so that we can properly relate to our women and children. They need and deserve our love, affection and understanding, but how can we properly give that to them and understand their feelings when we are too immature to admit our own.

Of course, there are times when we as men need to be strong, especially for our women and children. Our women need a man that's in touch with his feelings but is still strong enough to stand as a man. Our feelings as men have their place. Just make sure you understand that all quality men experience times when they feel pain and get hurt.

Manhood Statement
"I'm not ashamed to feel and admit hurt; understanding my hurts makes me better!"

"I am hurt and lonely. Turn to me, and show me mercy."
~ Psalms 25:16 ERV

* * *

"You cannot acquire experience by making experiments. You cannot create experience. You must undergo it."
~ Albert Camus

#46
Learn From Your Hurts

As males it's important to be honest when we experience hurt. It's only when we're truly honest, accept our hurts and admit our disappointments that we can truly learn from them and grow stronger. Sometimes we experience hurt because of expectations we shouldn't have had or because we trusted someone that didn't deserve it. Our hurts may also be a result of something stupid or selfish we've done. So, in some cases, the hurt we feel is in direct response to our own actions. At these times, it's important to be mature enough to learn from them.

Sometimes the hurt and disappointment we feel is based in some underlying fear, which may be displayed as anger. It's important that we take the time to judge our feelings of hurt to find the real core issues. As we become better men, let's not run from our hurts but be honest and learn from them.

Manhood Statement

"I am mature enough to be honest about my fears and I examine and learn from them!"

"The Lord does what is fair. He brings justice to all who have been hurt by others."
~ Psalms 103:6 ERV

***

"Our wounds are often the openings into the best and most beautiful part of us."
~ David Richo

#47
Accept Hurt To Heal

A very important reason to acknowledge and accept hurt is because it's the only way to truly heal. If you scar your arm and then act as if the scar isn't real, you'll probably spend a lot of time bumping it over and over again keeping it from healing properly. It's only after you accept and are honest about the scar, cover it up and protect it, that it's truly allowed to heal.

Likewise, as males, we must be honest about the things that hurt us. We must accept them; learn from them and heal from them so that we can grow and become better as men. Then we'll be in position to understand and help those around us. One of the most important outcomes of the pain that we will experience in our lives, is how we use it to help someone else.

Manhood Statement
"I'm honest and mature enough about the disappointments and pains I experience to learn from them and help someone else!"

"Yes, if you forgive others for the wrongs they do to you, then your Father in heaven will also forgive your wrongs."
~ Matthew 6:14 ERV

* * *

"The only way out of the labyrinth of suffering is to forgive."
~ John Green

#48
Forgiving Hurts Benefits You

Everyone has experienced some type of hurt that's hard to forgive. However, despite how difficult, we must forgive any person or situation that may have caused us pain, even if the person is us. The forgiveness we give isn't because we like the hurt, or because we're opening our lives up for it to happen again. We forgive because it benefits us.

Our minds will consistently replay for us the things that we've experienced in life; both the good and the bad. When a bad experience is replayed in our minds, our emotions cause us to experience the effects of the hurtful situation over and over again. This is why forgiveness is so important. It stops the painful situations we've experienced in life from continuing to replay in our minds and ends the cycle of the negative emotions that we experience as a result of them.

Manhood Statement
"I forgive to make sure I'm not reliving old pains that can affect my future!"

"Help me understand your instructions, and I will think about your wonderful teachings."
~ Psalms 119:27 ERV

* * *

"To find fulfillment...don't exist with life - embrace it."
~ Jim Beggs

X
ADJUSTMENTS

"The Adjustments Of Manhood"

adjustment [uh-juhst-muh nt] noun - the act of adjusting; adaptation to a particular condition, position, or purpose: the state of being adjusted; orderly relation of parts or elements: a device, as a knob or lever, for adjusting: the act of bringing something into conformity with external requirements: harmony achieved by modification or change of a position:

When it comes to working toward manhood, you will have to know when and where to make adjustments. We all run into situations where we may need to learn to view a situation or issue in a slightly different way before we can make the proper adjustments needed to help move us toward manhood.

"Stop doing anything evil and do good, and you will always have a place to live."
~ Psalms 37:27 ERV

* * *

"I'm not judging people; I'm judging their actions. It's the same type of distinction that I try to apply to myself, to judge, but not be judgmental."
~ Jeff Melvoin

#49
Good Intentions & Good Actions

Intentions are good but end up worthless when they are not followed through with good actions. Good intentions that are never supported by good actions, are nothing more than useless thoughts. As a man of manhood, it's important that you aren't full of good intentions and never express good actions.

The people around you will evaluate the type of quality man you are, not based on your "good intentions", because intentions are internal and unseen. People will know you're a good man by your "good actions." So be a quality man of manhood and be like Nike; "Just Do It!" As you pursue manhood, your actions will show others who you are by the good they see displayed in your life.

Manhood Statement
"As a man of manhood, I purposely make sure that my good intentions are seen by the world around me as good actions!"

"My people are destroyed because they have no knowledge."
~ Hosea 4:6 ERV

***

"Confidence is ignorance. If you're feeling cocky, it's because there's something you don't know."
~ Eoin Colfer

#50
Ignorance Will Cost You

Strong men know that they're responsible for their actions and don't use ignorance as an excuse. Because you didn't know it, doesn't change its effects in your life. So, ignorance will cost you. It would benefit us greatly to learn as much as we can about the areas of our lives that affect us the most.

The things we do in ignorance still impact us and those around us. It's important that we increase in learning and understanding to purposely minimize our areas of ignorance. Also, most of the time, we don't know, what we don't know. A constant state of learning will diminish areas of ignorance in your life. As you grow and become a better man, it's important to accept the things you don't know and continue to learn so your areas of ignorance don't drastically cost you and those around you.

Manhood Statement
"I accept responsibility for ignorance and increase my understanding in every area!"

"For as he thinks in his heart, so is he."
~ Proverbs 23:7 ERV

* * *

"The world as we have created it is a process of our thinking. It cannot be changed without changing our thinking."
~ Albert Einstein

#51
Change Your Thoughts & Actions

Our actions are mostly a direct result of our thoughts and beliefs. For example, when we think negatively about someone, we'll then treat them negatively. However, when we have positive thoughts about someone, we'll treat them positively. It's our thoughts that determine our actions. It takes a high level of maturity to recognize that if we want to change our actions, we must first change the thoughts that cause our actions.

As you develop into a better man, take the time to change the negative actions in your life by changing the negative thoughts that lead towards those actions. The ability to change the thoughts that lead towards our actions is the type of behavior that will distinguish quality men from childish males.

Manhood Statement
"I purposely change the negative thoughts and beliefs that lead me towards negative and destructive actions!"

"My people, listen to my teachings. Listen to what I say."
~ Psalms 78:1 ERV

* * *

"Lots of people talk to animals. Not very many listen though, that's the problem."
~ Benjamin Hoff

#52
Learn to Listen

We as men can be very stubborn and prideful at times, especially towards those closest to us, like our women and children. Sometimes we feel like we know what needs to happen and everyone just needs to listen. But the thing that our women and children need along with our leadership is our loving hearts. One way we express a loving heart is by truly listening to what others have to say.

Listening is an expression of love. When you love someone, you honor their words and feelings. When we ignore and dishonor our women and children's words and feelings, we express to them that they don't matter. To truly display manhood, take the time to listen to those around you so that they truly feel honored and valued. Taking the time and learning to listen expresses love and honor in ways that your words can't.

Manhood Statement
"I show love to my woman and children by learning how to truly hear and listen!"

"Change your hearts! And show by the way you live that you have changed."
~ Matthew 3:8 ERV

***

"Yesterday I was clever, so I wanted to change the world. Today I am wise, so I am changing myself."
~ Rumi

#53
The Strength To Change

Why do so many males continue to repeat destructive behaviors, continue to perform perverted acts or maintain and often expand their negative habits and beliefs? Because, change takes strength. It's not easy to change, even if it would benefit and enhance your life. It's not easy to change the life you have, even if you really want a better one. If it was easy, everyone would be like Nike and "Just Do It!" When a person wants to change but doesn't, it's most likely not because they don't think it would benefit them, but because they lack the strength to actually do the work involved to change.

If you want the strength needed to change, you'll need a desire to change that's stronger than all of the obstacles that are in your way. If you place the "YOU that you WANT to be" above the "YOU that you ARE," the strength to change is in your view.

Manhood Statement
"I develop the strength to change so that I display manhood in every area of my life!"

"With patience, you can make anyone change their thinking, even a ruler. Gentle speech is very powerful."
~ **Proverbs 25:15 ERV**

* * *

"Repentance is a lifetime self-improvement."
~ Toba Beta

#54
The Strength To Repent

During your process of becoming a better man, you'll need the strength to repent. The "Naves Topic Bible Concordance" describes "repentance" as, "A complete reversal of one's attitude and values." If you're driving heading north on the highway, "repentance" would be making a complete U-turn and heading south. So, when you "repent" you have a complete reversal of direction.

Repentance is needed to grow from a *selfish child* to a *selfless man*. Selfish and selfless are two completely different destinations, with two completely different outcomes. Now let's be clear, the words "I'm sorry," or "I apologize." aren't true repentance unless there's a change in the actions and beliefs that caused you to do something that needed to be apologized for in the first place.

Manhood Statement
"I have the strength to repent and change my direction towards what is right!"

"Good people are like budding palm trees. They grow strong like the cedar trees of Lebanon."
~ Psalms 92:12 ERV

* * *

"The important thing is this: to be able at any moment to sacrifice what we are for what we could become."
~ Charles Du Bos

#55
Growth Requires Consistency

You may find yourself missing it here and there as you grow into a better man. The key is to be consistent in the direction of quality manhood that you're going in. Consistency is vital if you're ever going to reach a specific destination. So, you'll need to consistently keep your ultimate goal of quality manhood in sight if you are ever going to obtain it.

As you're climbing a mountain, if you want to keep moving up, you must keep looking up. If you keep looking down, your reaching the top would take much longer, if at all, because of your lack of focus. Likewise, if you're ever going to become a better man and develop quality manhood, you'll need to consistently learn, grow, move, practice and live the principles that will make you better. It's your consistency that'll move you from a life of selfish childhood to living a life of quality manhood.

Manhood Statement
"I make a decision to be consistent in my growth towards manhood!"

"He said, "Whoever wants to be the most important must make others more important than themselves. They must serve everyone else."
~ Mark 9:35 ERV

"There is no greater joy nor greater reward than to make a fundamental difference in someone's life."
~ Sister Mary Rose McGeady

#56
Greatness By Helping Others

A saying went something like this: *"I don't want to be good, I want to be great. The only way to be great is to live a life that impacts others."* If you think of the greatest people in history, they include people who lived a life that affected others. Greatness cannot be contained; it expands and affects others.

We all have a sphere of influence that we can use to impact someone either positively or negatively. So, is your life helping or hurting others; making someone better or making someone worse. Is it taking someone higher or bringing them lower? If you take the influence you have in your life and have a great impact on someone else, greatness is the result. So, become great as a result of the positive and beneficial impact you have in the life of someone else.

Manhood Statement
"I display greatness in my life by the positive and beneficial impact that I purposely have on the life of others!"

"Jesus answered, "If any of you has a sheep and it falls into a ditch on the Sabbath day, you will take the sheep and help it out of the ditch."
~ Matthew 12:11 ERV

"Anyone who has never made a mistake has never tried anything new."
~ Albert Einstein

XI
MISTAKES

"Mistakes Enhance Manhood"

mis·take [mi-steyk] noun - an error in action, calculation, opinion, or judgment caused by poor reasoning, carelessness, insufficient knowledge, etc. a misunderstanding or misconception.

As we go through this process of becoming better males, we'll have to keep in mind that we are still growing and developing. So, with that mistakes are liable to happen. It's part of the process. Making mistakes is something that everyone will need to embrace and accept to continue the process of growth and development. Understanding this is vital for any male who wants to truly become a quality man.

"Many plans are in a man's mind, but it is the Lord's purpose for him that will stand."
~ Proverbs 19:21 AMP

* * *

"Ignorant men don't know what good they hold in their hands until they've flung it away."
~ Sophocles

#57
Bad Results, Aren't Always Bad

Let's make an assumption about the type of male you are if you're reading this and say that you desire to be a quality male and don't live your life looking for ways to steal, rob, kill or hurt others. So, there will be times when you'll try to do something positive or beneficial, but the result you get is negative and not what you hoped for. However, a bad or negative result isn't necessarily bad, if you use it to learn what *not* to do.

Thomas Edison tried 10,000 times to make the lightbulb, but he never gave up, because each bad result, taught him what didn't work. You can view your negative results as learning experiences that teach you what not to do and what doesn't work, if you let them. As you strive to become a better man, don't be discouraged by bad results, use them as the building blocks of your success.

Manhood Statement
"I view my bad results as learning experiences towards my success!"

"You who are ignorant, learn to be wise. You who are foolish, get some common sense."
~ Proverbs 8:5 ERV

* * *

"The world is wide, and I will not waste my life in friction when it could be turned into momentum."
~ Frances Willard

#58
Try, Fail, Learn & Try Again

The quality principles that we discuss here may require some effort to truly understand them and make them a working part of your life. Some males may get them instantly, while others may need to try them, fail at them, reread them, talk about them and try them again, before they can truly grasp them.

If you really want to become a better man, it will cost you. Just like it takes resistance and consistency to build muscle, it will take time and development to become a stronger man. It takes time, effort, practice and work to move from childhood into manhood. So, take the time and try and fail, learn from your failure, and then try again. Let's stress the point of "learn" here. Don't just "try, try and try again" without learning. If you don't ever "learn" your "tries" may get you nowhere.

Manhood Statement
"I continue to try while I learn from every failure, so that I can try again!"

"Listen to my teaching and be wise; don't ignore what I say."
~ Proverbs 8:33 ERV

"Facts are stubborn things; and whatever may be our wishes, our inclinations, or the dictates of our passion, they cannot alter the state of facts and evidence."
~ John Adams

#59
Ask, What Have I Learned?

No matter what situation or circumstance you face in life, learn from it. Whenever a situation doesn't end favorably, take time to judge and evaluate the it to learn all you can from it, if you ever want to avoid repeating it in the future.

At the end of every situation, ask yourself, "What have I learned from this?" Evaluate every situation completely to find out what you could have done differently. It may also be a good idea to discuss the situation with someone else of good character to see if they have a different perspective that you may not have seen. Every situation has something to teach us, if we don't find out what it is, we may end up repeating the "bad" we don't want, or we may have no idea how to repeat the "good" we do want.

Manhood Statement
"In every situation, I ask myself "What have I learned?" to make sure I'm always learning how to become a better man!"

"If one person falls, the other person can reach out to help. But those who are alone when they fall have no one to help them."
~ Ecclesiastes 4:10 ERV

"I cannot teach anybody anything. I can only make them think."
~ Socrates

#60
Learn From Others

There's always someone to learn from. So, find a mentor or quality man that will hold you accountable to becoming a better man. Experience is a great teacher, but you could learn from others mistakes and avoid making them yourself, if you're smart enough to listen. Learning from others can help you to examine your own mistakes and make the needed adjustments.

Don't try and be an island to yourself. Look to learn from someone who has been where you are and has learned what you want to know. It's a sign of wisdom if you can do so. But again, make sure the person you learn from is actually teaching you something that will benefit you and your future. So, make it a point to learn from others and let them teach you the things they have learned as you develop into manhood.

Manhood Statement
"I'm strong enough to find quality mentors and examples to learn from!"

"Yes, God loved the world so much that he gave his only Son, so that everyone who believes in him would not be lost but have eternal life."
~ John 3:16 ERV

"His life was gentle, and the elements so mix'd in him that Nature might stand up and say to all the world 'This was a man!'"
~ William Shakespeare

XII
LOVE

"True Love Of Manhood"

Love [luhv] noun - a profoundly tender, passionate affection for another person. a feeling of warm personal attachment or deep affection, as for a parent, child, or friend: a person toward whom love is felt; beloved person; sweetheart: verb - (used with object), loved, loving: to have love or affection for: to have a profoundly tender, passionate affection for (another person): to have a strong liking for;

As we grow into better men, we must adjust our thinking to understand the principles that really display quality manhood. I think that the most important principle to understand and embrace is the concept of unconditional love. Unfortunately, most men have been taught that love is more for the women than the men. But love is not just for women, a quality man will lead his woman by his love. But how can he truly lead her in something he believes is only for women or that he doesn't understand?

"Dear friends, we should love each other, because love comes from God. Everyone who loves has become God's child. And so everyone who loves knows God."
~ 1 John 4:7 ERV

**

"Nobody has ever measured, not even poets, how much the heart can hold."
~ Zelda Fitzgerald

#61
A Man's Unconditional Love

When we live a life that purposely gives unconditional love, that love that we give to others makes us greater because we are then in a position to receive love in return. The same way God gives unconditional love to us and receives love back from us; when a man loves his woman, children and others with unconditional love, he'll receive it back.

When love is shared from an unconditional heart, you not only experience the joy of sharing love, but you plant the seeds of love that will grow up and return to you. Love helps us grow together. It's the source of all lasting relationships. When a man takes the time to give his woman unconditional love, it will allow them to become truly "one" in body, soul and spirit in a way that no other union can match.

Manhood Statement
"I give unconditional love to my woman, children and others knowing I will receive unconditional love in return!"

"Now which do you prefer? Shall I come to you with a rod of correction, or with love and in a spirit of gentleness?"
~ I Corinthians 4:21 AMP

* * *

"Good men must be affectionate men."
~ Samuel Richardson

" # #62
Lead With Your Love

Have you known a man that labeled himself as "the head", but his wife, children or others never really followed him? This may be because it's easier to follow someone that you know loves you, than it is to follow a person with a position. A person that loves and honors you can be trusted not to make selfish decisions that only benefits them and their position.

Leading with love is the quickest and most effective way to get someone to follow you. Not because you're "the man in charge," but because you're "a man of love". Your love will help you lead. Your love will help you relate. Your love will draw you closer with the people around you. However, if you're motivated by your own selfish desires and needs, your selfish mindset won't help others follow you, it'll just push them away.

Manhood Statement

"I purposely lead others with the love and honor that I have for them!"

"The whole law is made complete in this one command: 'Love your neighbor the same as you love yourself.'"
~ Galatians 5:14 ERV

* * *

"The wisest men follow their own direction."
~ Euripides

#63
Love For Yourself

You can't give love to others, if there's no love inside you. To have love inside of you, you must know that you deserve to be loved. Some of the unhappiest and unpleasant people you'll ever meet are the people who don't feel loved. And the people that don't feel loved, probably have people around them that love them dearly. However, for some reason, they just don't love themselves.

A man that truly possesses love for himself, can easily give love away. No matter what people have said about you, what you've done or where you've come from, you deserve to be loved. There's some woman or some child somewhere that needs a quality man, with love in his heart to provide them with comfort and support. You're valuable and important and someone needs you to love yourself, so you can give love away.

Manhood Statement
"As a display of manhood, I purposely love others with the love that's within me!"

"The person that doesn't love does not know God, for God is love."
~ 1 John 4:8 CEB

* * *

"Conscience is the inner voice that warns us somebody may be looking."
~ H. L. Mencken

#64
Love For God

It's been said, *"The person who doesn't love does not know God, because God is love."* To be a man of love, you must first connect with love, and God is love. No matter your race, beliefs, or background spend some personal alone time and speak with the Source of Love: God. It's through a personal relationship with Him that you can and will feel the true source of love for you, and love in you.

Whether or not you've ever spoken to Him, I ask that you do so now in a way that's not scripted, that's not religious and that's not formal. Approach Him as a child before a Father, and reach out to Him in love and honesty. If you reach out to Him, I promise in some way, He'll make Himself real and reach back to you. As a male, we will only reach manhood with the help and love of the One who made us to be males, Our Creator.

Manhood Statement
"I take the time to reach out to God and connect with His love for me!"

"For all that is in the world–the lust of the flesh [craving for sensual gratification] and the lust of the eyes [greedy longings of the mind] and the pride of life [assurance in one's own resources or in the stability of earthly things]–these do not come from the Father but are from the world [itself]."
~ 1 John 2:16 AMP

* * *

"Darkness cannot drive out darkness: only light can do that. Hate cannot drive out hate: only love can do that."
~ Martin Luther King Jr.

#65
Real Love, Not Temporary Lust

The most beneficial relationships we will have in life, will be based in unconditional love. True unconditional love rejuvenates, gives strength and adds real meaning to our relationships and life. True love can last forever if it's mutual and each member puts the needs of the other above their own.

On the other hand, lust is short term, selfish and unfulfilling in nature. Lust provides an immediate gratification that's never truly satisfied; lust always wants more and more. To become a quality man, you must have quality relationships that are based in true love not in acts of temporary lust. Little boys seek to please themselves in any way they can. However, a quality man, that displays manhood, lives in a way that brings meaning and happiness to the relationships that he has with others.

Manhood Statement
"I seek to experience relationships based in lasting love and not temporary lust!"

"And now, my daughter, fear not. I will do for you all you require, for all my people in the city know that you are a woman of strength (worth, bravery, capability)."
~ Ruth 3:11 AMP

* * *

"You educate a man; you educate a man. You educate a woman; you educate a generation."
~ Brigham Young

XIII
WOMEN

"Manhood Honors Women"

woman [woo m-uh n] noun - the female human being, as distinguished from a girl or a man: an adult female person: the nature, characteristics, or feelings often attributed to women; womanliness: a sweetheart or paramour; mistress.

It's been said, "You'll know the type of man he is, by looking at his woman." How a man treats his woman is the purest representation of what type of man he is. His woman will experience him when he's not acting or pretending to be something he's not. She'll experience who he truly is behind closed doors at times of ease and times of conflict. If he can give honor and love to his woman, then he's a man of respect and quality standards. If he abuses and mistreats his woman, he's a man of immaturity and low standards. If you want to know whether you're living by the principles of manhood, judge your treatment of the woman closest to you.

"A capable, intelligent, and virtuous woman—who is he who can find her?"
~ Proverbs 31:10 AMP

* * *

"Whatever you give a woman, she will make greater. Give her sperm, she'll give you a baby. Give her a house, she'll give you a home. Give her groceries, she'll give you a meal. Give her a smile, she'll give you her heart. She multiplies and enlarges what is given to her. Give her any crap, be ready to receive a ton of s#@*!"
~ Erick S. GrayThurber

#66
Recognize Her Worth & Purpose

It's not possible to become a better man, without recognizing the worth of the ground by which "life" enters the world; a woman. A woman is a living incubator. She's created to receive from a man and give back to him something greater. Physically, women have the receiving area, and men have the giving member. When a man gives her love and affection, he receives honor and respect; but if a man gives a woman dishonor and abuse, he'll receive it back, in a much greater form; and not necessarily from her, but "life" itself will fight for her; be it her Heavenly Father, her natural father, her brother or the law.

Women are a gift given to men for us to cherish and care for. When loved properly, we men receive all we want and need from them. When we respect and honor a woman's purpose, we can truly benefit from them.

Manhood Statement
"I honor a woman's purpose and cherish her without taking her for granted!"

"...husbands should live with your wives in an understanding way, since they are weaker than you. You should show them respect, because God gives them the same blessing he gives you — the grace of true life. Do this so that nothing will stop your prayers from being heard."
~ 1 Peter 3:7 ERV

* * *

"When a man strikes another man, he better have a good reason. There is never a good reason for a man to strike a woman."
~ Dixie Waters

#67
Mistreating Her, Impacts You

As with anything in life, it must be properly maintained, to run successfully. The same goes for our relationships. If we as men expect our women to perform at peak levels, we must make sure they have all that they need to do so. If you as a man, only use and take from your woman for your own needs, and never put back into her what she needs, it's only a matter of time before she'll become empty. Not necessarily because there's something wrong with her, more than how you're treating her.

As a quality man, please understand that your mistreatment of your woman will cost "you" her heart and your relationship. Don't let your mistreatment of your woman, impact you, by opening the door for another quality man, to show her how valuable she is, and do for her what you were too immature or selfish to do.

Manhood Statement
"I make sure that I'm giving my woman the love, attention and affection she needs!"

"The wife does not have power over her own body. Her husband has the power over her body. And the husband does not have power over his own body. His wife has the power over his body."
~ 1 Corinthians 7:4 ERV

***

"Women and men have to fight together to change society - and both will benefit... Partnership, not dependence, is the real romance in marriage."
~ Muriel Fox

#68
Your Strength Benefits Her

As men, we've been created to be naturally stronger than women, generally speaking of course. There's a reason for that; so that we are equipped to cover them, serve them, protect them and care for them. However, it seems that some males don't understand this and use their strength to misuse and abuse women and children in childish, selfish and destructive ways.

A quality man uses his strength to benefit his woman; to make her feel safe and secure; and to express his love for her. If you're a male that abuses women and children, you need to truly connect to the purpose of your strength and seek to expand your thinking. Get help and understanding from quality men on what it means to be a male that uses his strength in ways that honor woman and children, not to abuse them.

Manhood Statement
"My physical strength is used to benefit women and children and not to hurt them!"

"Be happy with your own wife. Enjoy the woman you married while you were young."
~ Proverbs 5:18 ERV

* * *

"Where there is love, there is life."
~ Mahatma Gandhi

#69
Lead Her And Please Her

A quality man doesn't always do what his woman wants, more than always has a heart to serve her and do what's best for her and their relationship. A woman wants a man that can take the lead, but with the love, kindness and respect that she deserves. If you maintain a heart of respect and love for your woman, you'll be able to lead her and please her at the same time.

Most women wouldn't have no problem following a man that she knows loves and honors her. If she does, there's other issues going on that need to be addressed and talked about immediately. Make it a point to love and lead her and you'll simultaneously be pleasing to her. Make her feel valued and cared for and she will, most likely, have no problem submitting and following that love.

Manhood Statement
"I am a quality man that loves and honors my woman as I serve and lead her!"

"And said, For this reason a man shall leave his father and mother and shall be united firmly (joined inseparably) to his wife, and the two shall become one flesh?"
~ Matthew 19:5 ERV

"We touch other people's lives simply by existing. "
~ J. K. Rowling

#70
Sex Isn't Just Physical

Our society has minimized sex to a common and casual act of fun and pleasure. However, when you join your body to another person, it's not "sex," its "sexual intercourse". It's the joining of the male essence and the female essence in a very special and unique way of spirit, soul and body.

Sex is not just a one-time interaction; it's a lasting bond created through the sexual intercourse, or interchange, of two spirits through sex. So, the more sex you have, the more of your essence you give away and the less of it you have left. This is why so many people feel empty. They've given so much of themselves away through meaningless sex. This is why it's so important to join with the wife that you plan to spend the rest of your life with so that every sexual encounter builds a meaningful relationship and draws you closer together.

Manhood Statement
"I understand that sex isn't just physical, it's spiritual and has a lasting effect!"

"But he knows not that the shades of the dead are there, and that her invited guests are [already sunk] in the depths of Sheol (the lower world, Hades, the place of the dead)."
~ Proverbs 9:18 ERV

* * *

"Research found that marriages in which one person has a porn problem or sexual compulsion are often plagued by less intimacy and sensitivity, as well as more anxiety, secrecy, isolation, and dysfunction in the relationship."
~ FightTheNewDrug.org"

#71
PORN Destroys Lives & Love

One of the biggest lies we've ever been told, is that there's nothing wrong with porn. Porn destroys lives, relationships and distorts true love. There's extensive research about "the effects of porn" online and through sites like "fightthenewdrug.org" which explain that:

• Porn Affects You Like A Drug: When you watch porn, the brain is rewired, making you want to watch it again and again, whether you want to or not you begin to crave it.

• Porn Changes The Brain: Like other drugs, porn floods the brain with dopamine and changes the makeup of your brain which creates an increased appetite for porn.

• Porn Effects Behavior: Viewing violent and disrespectful porn sex acts causes you to begin to see them as normal. As a result, new twisted desires are created within you.

Manhood Statement
"I purposely avoid porn so that it doesn't negatively affect my life and the people around me that I love!"

"Depart from evil and do good; and you will dwell forever [securely]."
~ Psalm 37:27 ERV

* * *

"He who labors diligently need never despair; for all things are accomplished by diligence and labor."
~ Menander

XIV
APPLICATION

"Apply Manhood Principles"

application [ap-li-key-shuh n] noun - the act of putting to a special use or purpose: the application of common sense to a problem: the special use or purpose to which something is put: the quality of being usable for a particular purpose or in a special way; relevance:

No matter what principles you learn, if you don't take the time to actually apply them, they'll never become real and benefit your life. In school, it's great for us to attend every class, listen closely and sit right in front of the teacher, but it's not until we actually pass the test that we'll really benefit from all that we've learned. It's important that we, as men, not only learn how to become better, but that we display quality manhood in our lives for the whole world around us to see and benefit from it.

"[Charge them] to do good, to be rich in good works, to be liberal and generous of heart, ready to share [with others],"
~ 1 Timothy 6:18 AMP

***

"Shallow men believe in luck. Strong men believe in cause and effect."
~ Ralph Waldo Emerson

#72
Let Your Actions Speak

There's a saying, "Actions speak louder than words." Let's add to that and say that your actions will either: agree with your words to prove them right; disagree with your words to prove them wrong; or, speak on their own without any words being needed. You can tell your wife you love her over and over, but if your actions are selfish, unfaithful and disrespectful, you're actually telling her that you really don't love her at all or that you have no idea what real love is.

If you're a man of character, your actions will speak. Many times, words aren't needed when the right actions are displayed on a consistent basis. As you pursue manhood, be the type of man that allow both your words and your actions to tell your woman, your children and the world around you the type of quality man you are.

Manhood Statement
"I live in a way that both my words and my actions display the quality man I am!"

"Let a person examine himself, then, and so eat of the bread and drink of the cup."
~ 1 Corinthians 11:28 ESV

* * *

"It is not for me to judge another man's life. I must judge, I must choose, I must spurn, purely for myself. For myself, alone."
~ Hermann Hesse

#73
Judge Yourself Consistently

A judge is "a public official appointed to evaluate and render verdicts in a court of law based on evidence." However, *to judge* is "to form an opinion or to reach a conclusion based on evidence." If you want to become a better man, it's important to judge yourself on a consistent basis to make sure that what you say and do truly displays love and honor. To properly judge yourself, you'll need to first understand the principles of manhood and then examine your words and actions to see if you're truly living by those principles.

We need to consistently judge our words and actions to evaluate whether or not our lives truly display quality manhood. By judging yourself consistently, you'll ensure that you are always becoming a better man and are a living example of quality manhood.

Manhood Statement
"I judge my motives, words and actions to make sure I display quality manhood!"

"The one who states his case first seems right, until the other comes and examines him."
~ Proverbs 18:17 ESV

* * *

"You can't lie to your soul."
~ Irvine Welsh, Porno

#74
Judge Yourself Honestly

A quality man is always mindful of areas of "self-deception." Self-deception is when we believe something to be true about ourselves that's really not, or when we're unable to see our own faults. We can avoid self-deception by always being honest with ourselves about our own faults and weaknesses, and by listening to the constructive criticisms of quality people.

So, make sure that any self-judgments are always honest and true. If you're not going to judge yourself honestly, you do yourself a great injustice. If you don't think you can judge yourself honestly, don't judge yourself at all. Find someone you trust who will tell you the truth about yourself. Give them the right to judge your actions and listen to what they say. It's this type of honest input that will help you become a better man.

Manhood Statement
"I judge myself honestly and make the proper adjustments towards manhood!"

"Practice these things, immerse yourself in them, so that all may see your progress."
~ 1 Timothy 4:15 ESV

* * *

"I have always thought the actions of men the best interpreters of their thoughts."
~ John Locke

#75
Practice Towards Perfection

Let's be honest, no matter how hard you work towards becoming a better man, you'll slip up at times. None of us have arrived, so none of us should dare act like we have. We all need to continue practicing at becoming better men. Since God is patient with us, we should be patient with ourselves.

As you're becoming better, don't give up on yourself. The more you stay focused on becoming a better man, the more it'll become a reality. When you mess up, act childish and/or screw up, apologize to those you've effected, learn from your mistake and then get up and keep growing. Developing into quality manhood is a lifelong process so keep moving. Don't try and do it alone. Find other friends, brothers and mentors that are in the process of becoming better as well that you can glean strength from as you grow.

Manhood Statement
"I keep practicing quality principles and never give up on becoming a better man!"

"Wisdom will help you live longer; she will add years to your life."
~ Proverbs 9:11 ERV

* * *

"The reason I talk to myself is because I'm the only one whose answers I accept."
~ George Carlin

#76
Let It Out & Talk

One thing we as males often find it hard to do, is talk. We tend to keep stuff bottled up inside and try to work out our issues on our own. This may sound like a good idea, but this practice has caused a lot of males' problems. For example, women, on average, live longer than men do because they're much more open about sharing their areas of stress. By opening up and talking, they find mental relief and support.

However, males have been told not to feel or express emotions; just keep them inside. Not getting in touch with our emotions doesn't mean we don't have them; we just aren't expressing them and end up carrying internal stress as a result. By talking about our issues, we can find the support and counsel needed to grow. Letting out your concerns may be one of the best decisions you'll ever make.

Manhood Statement
"I express my concerns to quality people instead of keeping them inside!"

"...give, and it will be given to you. Good measure, pressed down, shaken together, running over, will be put into your lap. For with the measure you use it will be measured back to you."
~ Luke 6:38 ESV

"Insanity is doing the same thing, over and over again, but expecting different results."
~ Narcotics Anonymous

#77
Expect What You've Given

As quality men, we must be mature in our expectations of others and only expect from them, what we've given to them. We've all experienced times when someone gives to us something we don't deserve, like God's love. However, sometimes we place expectations on others and expect things from them that we quite frankly, don't deserve.

For example, when it comes to women, some males just expect women to just keep giving and giving, without them ever needing to give back. If we expect to keep receiving from anything, we must keep giving to it. When we go to the bank, we can't withdraw from an account unless a deposit was made into it first. A quality man will only expect to receive, what he's already given. So, if you want to receive something, make sure you've given it first.

Manhood Statement
"I'm mature enough to know that I need to give if I ever want to receive!"

"Let the wise hear and increase in learning, and the one who understands obtain guidance,"
~ Proverbs 1:5 ESV

* * *

"Real joy comes not from ease or riches or from the praise of men, but from doing something worthwhile."
~ Sir Wilfred Grenfell

#78
Understand And Control

If you're ignorant about car repair, you'd be left stranded if your car ever broke down. However, if you understood how to fix cars, you'd be able to repair it yourself with the proper parts. When situations arise in our lives that we don't understand, they have the ability to control us simply because we don't fully understand them. However, proper understanding about the situations in our lives, helps us take control of them.

When we understand ourselves and why we do certain things, we can then take control of our thoughts, emotions and actions and are no longer controlled by them. It's important that we gain as much understanding as we can, on the things that happen and effect our lives so that we can take control of them and not be controlled by them.

Manhood Statement
"I understand and control my thoughts and emotions, and I'm not controlled by them!"

"But not so with you. Rather, let the greatest among you become as the youngest, and the leader as one who serves."
~ Luke 22:26 ESV

* * *

"Give a man a fire and he's warm for a day, but set fire to him and he's warm for the rest of his life."
~ Terry Pratchett

XV
LEADERSHIP

"Leading Others In Manhood"

leadership [lee-der-ship] noun - the position or function of a leader, a person who guides or directs a group: ability to lead: an act or instance of leading; guidance; direction:

One thing that I'm sure each of us have seen in one form or another is the effect that a male has on another male. The youth are constantly being influenced by who they're watching and/or emulating. Whether or not these people should be leading our boys or not isn't the issue; the fact is they're being followed by them. When a boy leads a boy, he stays a boy. When a man leads a boy, he becomes a man. It takes a quality man to create another quality man.

"Words from the wise bring praise, but words from a fool bring destruction."
~ Ecclesiastes 10:12 ERV

* * *

"I hope that in this year to come, you make mistakes. Because if you are making mistakes...you're Doing Something."
~ Neil Gaiman

#79
Share Your Mistakes

Our mistakes and experiences give us the ability to help others. No matter where you are in life, someone is watching you. You'll never know what male next to you, or behind you, may avoid unnecessary problems in his life, his relationships and his family by the experience and wisdom you share.

Don't let pride or embarrassment keep you from opening up your mistakes to those that can learn from them. If they decide not to listen and run head first into a brick wall, it won't be because you didn't tell them it was there. If you don't share your mistakes, just think about how many mistakes you could have avoided if someone would have shared with you. Share your mistakes and you can create a cycle of passing down some of the positive insights and wisdom you've learned to the next generation.

Manhood Statement
"I share my experiences and mistakes with others to help them avoid them if possible!"

"Whoever heeds instruction is on the path to life, but he who rejects reproof leads others astray."
~ Proverbs 10:17 ESV

"We must not allow the clock and the calendar to blind us to the fact that each moment of life is a miracle and mystery."
~ H. G. Wells

#80
See Yourself In Others

Oftentimes the issues we see in others, we've seen in ourselves. People have really not changed, what has changed is the standards and principles that we live by. So, when you see someone acting or doing something negative that you yourself used to do, that's not the time to point fingers and condemn them for how they are. On the contrary, it's the perfect time for us to be honest and remember how we used to be.

When we recognize immaturity in others, it can give us patience to show them love and teach them, if they let us. As we notice the needs of our boys and males of today, let's learn to look past their behavior to realize that the negative behaviors they display may be all they know. Maybe we'll then be in a better position to truly teach and help them develop into quality men.

Manhood Statement
"I remember how I used to be and show patience and love to others!"

"Judge not, and you will not be judged; condemn not, and you will not be condemned; forgive, and you will be forgiven;"
~ Luke 6:37 ESV

***

"Be the change that you wish to see in the world."
~ Mahatma Gandhi

#81
Understand, Not Condemn

We've all come from different situations and circumstances. Some may be similar, but very few are identical. So, when you look at someone else's life, seek to understand them and their situation without judging them. When we take the time to understand others and their situations, we're better equipped not to condemn them for their thoughts and behaviors.

As you develop true manhood, take the time to understand the people that you come in contact with, no matter what their behavior may be. An immature male will see a person from the outside, point fingers and condemn them. A quality man will seek to understand the people he comes in contact with. This focus will help and equip him to better understand their background and thoughts, without condemning their behavior.

Manhood Statement
"I understand a person's background, before I condemn their behavior!"

"The law of the Lord is perfect, reviving the soul; the testimony of the Lord is sure, making wise the simple;"
~ Psalms 19:7 ESV

"Make no little plans; they have no magic to stir men's blood. Make big plans, aim high in hope and work."
~ Daniel H. Burnham

#82
Share The Good

As men, we should share our wisdom with others. However, instead of wisdom, a lot of males are sharing twisted, selfish, immature and destructive behaviors and thoughts. As a result of this, our families, our morals and society continues to deteriorate as a whole.

It's the responsibility of every quality male to live his life in such a way, that he shares the good that benefits him, his wife, children and those around him. It's unfortunate that we as humans seem to thrive on the negative, much more than the positive. So, if you're going to share the good, it must be done on purpose. Don't allow the negative thoughts of others to go un-answered in your own mind and life. Be willing to purposely share the positive and uplifting aspects of your life whenever you can.

Manhood Statement
"I purposely share the good thoughts and concepts that'll benefit others, not the negative and destructive ones that won't!"

"As for you, brothers, do not grow weary in doing good."
~ 2 Thessalonians 3:13 ESV

* * *

"We are products of our past, but we don't have to be prisoners of it."
~ Rick Warren

XVI
GROWTH

"Constantly Grow In Manhood"

grow [groh] noun - to increase by natural development, as any living organism or part by assimilation of nutriment; increase in size or substance. to form and increase in size by a process of inorganic accretion, as by crystallization: to arise or issue as a natural development from an original happening,

The good things in life, worth having require work and consistency. Becoming a better man is not automatic. It will require work, effort, practice and time for the quality man you desire to be to manifest in your life. So, continue to grow in your quality manhood. Work to become better day by day. Only time will truly tell whether or not you are truly committed to growth as a man, and if those around you will ever benefit from the man of quality you're destined to be.

"Do not be conformed to this world, but be transformed by the renewal of your mind, that by testing you may discern what is the will of God, what is good and acceptable and perfect."
~ Romans 12:12 ESV

* * *

"We have, I fear, confused power with greatness."
~ Stewart L. Udall

#83
Set Your Own Trend

Webster's defines a "trend" as *"the general course or prevailing tendency; drift: style or vogue: to tend to take a particular direction; to emerge as a popular trend; to veer or turn off in a specified direction."* Of all these explanations, the last one stands out the most where it says, "to veer or turn off". We find trends around us everywhere from how we wear our clothes, what we listen to, and how we treat each other. But how many of the trends of our day, have "veered off" from a path that was beneficial, to one that's not.

As quality men, it's important that we don't follow every wind or trend that comes. Men of standard follow paths that lead them to prosperous relationships and lives. Don't be afraid to be different and create a trend of your own.

Manhood Statement
"I'm strong enough not to follow every trend that comes. I create my own trends that lead me towards success in life!"

"Finally, brothers, whatever is true, whatever is honorable, whatever is just, whatever is pure, whatever is lovely, whatever is commendable, if there is any excellence, if there is anything worthy of praise, think about these things."
~ Philippians 4:8 ESV

* * *

"Thoughts are like an open ocean, they can either move you forward within its waves, or sink you under deep into its abyss."
~Anthony Liccione

#84
Replace Negative Thoughts

Your thoughts will either lead you towards new successes or help you repeat cycles of failure. Purposely work to reject negative thoughts that can hinder you. Be mindful of negative influences that have the potential to create negative thoughts and concepts within your heart and mind.

Limit the time you spend around anyone that shares negative and destructive concepts that can hinder your progress. Also, be mindful of the negative thoughts and ideas that seem to pop into your mind at random. Don't just accept a thought because you have it. Make it a point to replace a negative thought, with a positive one, by speaking positive words. The positive words you speak and hear aloud from your own mouth, will replace any negative and destructive thoughts that you may hear in silence in your own mind.

Manhood Statement
"I purposely replace any negative thoughts and ideas, with positive ones!"

"Those who reject a command hurt themselves; those who respect a command will be rewarded."
~ Proverbs 13:13 ERV

* * *

"A brave man acknowledges the strength of other."
~ Veronica Roth

#85
Be Strong Enough To Get Help

Sometimes we men don't like to ask for help or directions, the problem with that is the longer we need help and don't ask for it, the longer we remain lost or heading in a wrong direction. We need to get over this especially if we expect our women and children to follow us. For the sake of those following him, a quality man gets help from wherever he needs too for those he loves.

If you find it hard to ask for help, you're most likely more concerned about your own self-image, than you are about what's best for those around you. In this case, change your focus off of you, to those that need you and get help to be the best you can be. There's always someone, somewhere that you can learn from. The answers you're looking for may be no further than in a trusted friend, a book or an internet search.

Manhood Statement
"I seek out help for my issues and concerns so that I'm always learning and growing!"

"Behold, how good and pleasant it is when brothers dwell in unity!"
~ Psalms 133:1 ESV

* * *

"Nearly all men can stand adversity, but if you want to test a man's character, give him power."
~ Abraham Lincoln

#86
Use The Strength Of Numbers

There're times when you'll need the strength that comes from numbers. It's good to be able to walk alone, but you can sometimes do more in a group. When the opportunity presents itself, use the strength that comes from a group to grow stronger. Just make certain that the focus and motive of the group is positive and not negative.

For example, gangs are normally effective in their group activities, the problem is what kinds of activities they're involved in. Find the strength that comes from positive groups like non-profit organizations that help and serve the community. This type of combined strength will help you develop relationships with others that have a mindset to give and not just take. It will also strengthen you in your path towards becoming a better man.

Manhood Statement
"I use the strength of positive groups to build my desire and ability to serve others and the community!"

"One person esteems one day as better than another, while another esteems all days alike. Each one should be fully convinced in his own mind."
~ Romans 14:5 ESV

"Be yourself; everyone else is already taken."
~ Oscar Wilde

#87
Live Positive Without Apology

Living a life of quality manhood won't be easy. As you strive to do, say and act like a quality man, you'll eventually run into the "haters". These will be boys, both young and old, that don't like what you're trying to do. Boys, who want to do the wrong things, want to mistreat women, want to take from others and want to talk about your desire to become a better man. To them I advise you to say a very polite, sincere and effective "Screw You!", and keep living your life of quality manhood without apology!

Don't apologize to any of the haters, hecklers or hazers! They're nothing but crabs in the barrel ready to get boiled and served up on the dinner plate of life, just like all the other childish, selfish and destructive males that take, instead of give. Ignore them, stay your course and become the best man you can be!

Manhood Statement
"I purposely live a life of quality manhood without apology or compromise!"

"Let brotherly love continue."
~ Hebrews 13:1 ESV

* * *

"If your life is really worth talking about, someone else will say it for you."
~ Eric M. Watterson

XVII
DISPLAY

"Display Manhood In Life"

display [dih-spley] verb - to show or exhibit; make visible; to reveal; to unfold; open out; spread out; exhibition;

A man can talk without ever saying a word. A quality man can let his presence speak for him without the need for words. A weaker man may need to explain who he is and what he stands for. A man that's truly operating in quality manhood doesn't need to say, "Here I Am.", it's evident. There's great strength in being able to let who you are speak. If who you are as a man is worth talking about, someone else will do it for you. If there's nothing good being said about you, it maybe because there's nothing good to be said.

"Beloved, if God so loved us, we also ought to love one another."
~ 1 John 4:11 ESV

* * *

"Love all, trust a few, do wrong to none."
~ William Shakespeare

#88
Love Strong; Love Hard

Despite what you've been told, or what you believe, love is by far, the strongest and most powerful emotion there is. It's through true unconditional love that parents sacrifice for their children, that people help others and give without expecting in return. But it's the opposite emotions of love, like selfishness, lust, racism, pride and hate that weaken our relationships and distort our intentions.

As you become a better man, purposely love hard. Don't just do good things for others, serve them from your heart. When you love your woman, your children, your marriage, and your life's purpose hard, you'll see life become truly impactful and effective. So, find those things in life you can love hard, and love strong! Love isn't for the weak; on the contrary, it's only for those males that are truly strong!

Manhood Statement
"I purposely find those things in life that I can love strong and love hard!"

"Who is that young woman? She shines out like the dawn. She is as pretty as the moon. She is as bright as the sun. She is as awesome as the stars in the sky."
~ Song of Songs 6:10 ERV

"It is not a lack of love, but a lack of friendship that makes unhappy marriages."
~ Friedrich Nietzsche

#89
Appreciate & Listen To Women

A lot of men don't seem to appreciate the differences and gifts in women. Women have gifts and abilities that we as men don't have. These differences aren't to separate us, but for us to truly join together, especially in marriage. Women have an internal insight, that will extend beyond what they see to a special internal knowing that men will often dismiss; it's a woman's intuition.

A quality man understands the importance of highly honoring, appreciating and listening to women, especially his wife. She'll have insight and understanding that will often only make sense to a man after he *doesn't* listen to her. He'll then wish he did, but maybe too prideful to admit it. Don't be like the multitude of males that run head first into brick walls, because they didn't appreciate and listen to their woman.

Manhood Statement
"I honor women by listening to their opinions, insights and understanding!"

"If you always try to be honest, murderers will hate you, but those who do what is right will want you to be their friend."
~ Proverbs 29:10 ERV

"Associate yourself with men of good quality if you esteem your own reputation for 'tis better to be alone than in bad company."
~ George Washington

#90
A Quality Man's Friend

When men hangout, there's a quality bond between brothers that's created. However, a quality man won't want to spend time with a man of weak values and goals. If you surround yourself with quality men that are striving to become better, your own sense of quality will grow as well. So, make sure that you're a man of standards and quality, so men of quality standards will welcome you.

The last thing a quality man wants around him is a childish, mouthy dude that loves the sound of his own voice. Purposely develop the type of character and integrity that other strong man of character and integrity would want as a friend. "Birds of a feather flock together." If a group of eagles don't want you around, it may be because you're a buzzard! Develop the quality mindset and lifestyle of an eagle, spread your wings and soar.

Manhood Statement
"My quality principles and character, makes strong men want me as a friend!"

"Love is patient and kind. Love is not jealous, it does not brag, and it is not proud. Love is not rude, it is not selfish, and it cannot be made angry easily. Love does not remember wrongs done against it."
~ 1 Corinthians 13:4-5 ERV

* * *

"When someone loves you, the way they talk about you is different. You feel safe and comfortable."
~ Jess C. Scott

#91
One In A Million

Our society has seemed to turn from one that honors others, especially women; to one that dishonors others, especially women. There was a time when the term "B#%CH" was highly unacceptable. However, it's become so acceptable that it's specifically inserted into popular music and entertainment. It's become so common in our society that some of our women actually seem surprised when they experience kindness from a man.

No matter what type of trend impacts the way males treat women in our society, our women still deserve to be treated by the beliefs and standards of a gentlemen, even if they don't expect it. It's this expectation that a quality man should exceed and surprise. You may be the only guy that a woman may encounter that treats her with honor and kindness. Don't miss the opportunity!

Manhood Statement
"I'm a one in a million man that some women may ever receive honor from!"

"Do everything in love."
~ 1 Corinthians 16:14 ERV

* * *

"When you connect to the silence within you, that is when you can make sense of the disturbance going on around you."
~ Stephen Richards

XVIII
LIFESTYLE

"The Lifestyle of Manhood"

lifestyle [lahyf-stahyl] noun - the habits, attitudes, tastes, moral standards, economic level, etc., that together constitute the mode of living of an individual or group. adjective - pertaining to or catering to a certain lifestyle:

As men, we need to find purpose in what we do. If we find purpose in becoming a better man, that purpose will help fuel us towards making proper decisions. Without a clearly defined purpose, we may find ourselves going around in circles, doing the same things over and over, because we have no clear goal. Without a clear goal, there's no standard to evaluate and judge our lifestyles by to determine if we are going in the right direction. As we pursue and develop into quality men, let's make sure that we are living a life that displays quality manhood.

"This message is from the Lord. "I have good plans for you. I don't plan to hurt you. I plan to give you hope and a good future.""
~ Jeremiah 29:11 ERV

* * *

"Find out who you are and do it on purpose."
~ Dolly Parton

#92
Understand Purpose

The word *"Purpose"* is defined as *"the reason for which something exists or is done, made, used, etc.;"* For example, the purpose for a car is to transport people from one point to another; it's a very cool benefit if it's also a Lamborghini. Purpose fulfills the ultimate goal that something is created and used for.

If the purpose for what you're doing only benefits you, it'll be short lived. On the other hand, if your purpose is intended to help others, it can last forever. Understanding purpose can fuel you towards completing it. For example, embracing your purpose for your wife and children to love, support and guard them will keep you doing, and not doing, everything needed to support them. When there's no beneficial purpose, pursuits are empty and fall short. Find purpose in what you do and watch your pursuits last.

Manhood Statement
"I seek to understand the purpose in the people and situations around me!"

"So let's try as hard as we can to do what will bring peace. Let's do whatever will help each other grow stronger in faith."
~ Romans 14:19 ERV

* * *

"We must live together as brothers or perish together as fools."
~ Martin Luther King Jr.

#93
Find Your Core Brothers

Every friend we have in life, is not the same. Some of our friends are actually more casual associates, however others may be close and trusted connections. Evaluate the people around you to make sure that you don't label someone a personal friend, that's actually more of a passing associate. Take the time to find those friends that you can truly label as brothers; let's call them your core brothers.

Your "Core Brothers" are a group of males, large or small, that share the same core principles and values that you have. They can be trusted with your intimate faults and weaknesses. They'll build you and not tear you down and wouldn't share your intimate faults or failures with others. They'll stand with you in a bind and expect you to do the same. Your core brothers can be trusted like family, because in their heart, they are.

Manhood Statement
"I take the time to find my core brothers that think and live in honor as I do!"

"Love each other in a way that makes you feel close like brothers and sisters. And give each other more honor than you give yourself."
~ Romans 12:10 ERV

"All that is necessary for the triumph of evil is that good men do nothing."
~ Edmund Burke

#94
Be Selfless, Not Selfish

To truly develop into a man that displays quality manhood, you must be selfless not selfish. When a person is selfless, the things they do and say are always intended to benefit someone else. Even when they use words of criticism, they're constructive because their goal is to help the other person. On the other hand, a person that's selfish is more concerned about themselves, what they desire and how to get it and not about anyone they may hurt in the process.

A selfish man is a lonely man. There may be people around him, however, he won't have any meaningful relationships because a selfish man will elevate himself above others and push them away. However, a selfless man will elevate people above himself and by doing, so he'll draw people to himself.

Manhood Statement
"As a quality man, I live a selfless life that draws people to me, not push them away!"

"A good (healthy) tree cannot bear bad (worthless) fruit, nor can a bad (diseased) tree bear excellent fruit [worthy of admiration]. Every tree that does not bear good fruit is cut down and cast into the fire. Therefore, you will fully know them by their fruits."
~ Matthew 7:18-20 AMP

"Trees that are slow to grow bear the best fruit."
~ Molière

#95
Focus On The Fruit

Of all the foods we eat, fruit has the ability to both sustain us and reproduce itself. Fruit nourishes our bodies when we eat it, but most fruits also have seeds within them, that can produce more fruit. In the same way, the types of words we speak and actions we take, will determine whether or not there's fruit produced in our lives.

A fruitful action will always benefit yourself and others, not only based on the love shown towards them, but also in what you'll receive in return. So, a fruitful act benefits the one the act is done towards and the one performing the act. On the other hand, un-fruitful acts like robbing, stealing, disrespect and abuse don't benefit anyone involved and creates victims and perpetrators. As a quality man, perform acts that have a positive and fruitful impact on others, and also on yourself.

Manhood Statement
"I perform fruitful acts that positively impact the lives of others and myself!"

"If we say we love God but hate any of our brothers or sisters in his family, we are liars. If we don't love someone we have seen, how can we love God? We have never even seen him."
~ 1 John 4:20 ERV

* * *

"A life lived helping and serving others is always interesting and beneficial."
~ Eric M. Watterson

#96
It's About Others

A great way to find purpose is to make sure our actions positively impact others. When they do, we not only enhance their lives, but our lives as well. By our actions, our lives are expanded by the impact we have on others. A life focused on oneself is limited because it only enhances one life; while a life focused on others is always expanding because it impacts and benefits many lives over and over.

Our lives should be used to help someone, to give support to someone, to train another male, to comfort a woman, to protect a child and to display God's love. Without this type of focus on others, you may find yourself asking, "Is this all there is?" or "Why am I here?" When you look for ways to benefit others, you'll always be growing into a better expression of quality manhood.

Manhood Statement
"I make sure that the words I say, and the things I do, benefit others in some way!"

"We pray that your kingdom will come — that what you want will be done here on earth, the same as in heaven."
~ Matthew 6:10 ERV

* * *

"When faith replaces doubt, when selfless service eliminates selfish striving, the power of God brings to pass His purposes."
~ Thomas S. Monson

#97
Acknowledge Your Creator

For you to truly understand who you are and the purpose you were created for, you should take the time to acknowledge your Creator, God the Father and His Son Jesus Christ. He loves you just the way you are and has a purpose for your life.

I realize that some people may not believe in God. However, your belief in Him doesn't remove Him from existence, it just removes His ability to exist in you. God knows and is concerned about you, your situation and your circumstances. If you take the time to get to know Him through His Son Jesus Christ, you are in line with discovering who you've been created to be. There's greatness inside you waiting for you to connect to it. The quality manhood that lives inside you will positively impact those around you and the entire world when you let it out.

Manhood Statement
"I acknowledge my Creator and allow Him to show me the purpose for my life!"

"Planning ahead will protect you, and understanding will guard you."
~ Proverbs 2:11 ERV

* * *

"You may be deceived if you trust too much, but you will live in torment if you do not trust enough."
~ Frank Crane

XIX
GUARD

"Guard Your Manhood"

guard [gahrd] verb - to keep safe from harm or danger; protect; watch over: to keep under close watch in order to prevent escape, misconduct, etc.: to keep under control or restraint as a matter of caution or prudence: to provide or equip with some safeguard or protective appliance, as to prevent loss, injury, etc.

As with anything in life that we really care for, there's an internal desire to guard and protect it. The things that we as quality men really care about, we guard and protect; like our cars, our time watching the game, our women, our children and our destiny. Make becoming a better man worth guarding and protecting. If your desire to develop into a better man for your wife, kids and family is important enough to you, you'll do whatever is needed to guard and protect it against any outside force that threatens it from becoming real in your life.

"Always remember this teaching. Don't forget it. It is the key to life, so guard it well."
~ Proverbs 4:13 ERV

* * *

"Men are born with two eyes, but only one tongue, in order that they should see twice as much as they say."
~ Charles Caleb Colton

#98
Guard Your Gates

How you feel, what you think and what you believe in your heart will determine the words you speak and the actions you take. To become better men, we must guard the entrances, or the gates, that lead to our hearts from negative influences and inputs.

To protect your heart, you must guard your ears (what you listen too); your mouth (what you say or agree with); and your mind (what you believe and what you think about). It's through these gates that concepts, opinions and beliefs enter your heart and effect your life. Evaluate what you hear and what you believe through the music, movies, videos, conversations, etc. you hear to make sure it always assists you in becoming a better man. Guard your gates and only accept thoughts and concepts into your heart that'll enhance your pursuit of quality manhood.

Manhood Statement
"I guard my gates and only accept in my heart what will make me a better man!"

"And He said to them, be careful what you are hearing. The measure [of thought and study] you give [to the truth you hear] will be the measure [of virtue and knowledge] that comes back to you–and more [besides] will be given to you who hear."
~ Mark 4:24 AMP

* * *

"Men are not prisoners of fate, but only prisoners of their own minds."
~ Franklin D. Roosevelt

#99
Guard Your Brother

Becoming a better man should be the goal of every male. One great way to make sure you're always getting better as a man, is to find another brother and you two help each other grow. Just like at the gym, it's easier to work out consistently and lift heavier when there's someone to push and spot you.

As you strive to become a better man, find another brother that's working to become better as well. Purposely support and guard your brother from those things that would threaten his development, and as a brother, expect him to help guard you from the things that may threaten yours. When you help guard your brother and support him in becoming a better man, not only are you assisting him, but you're also helping to reinforce the principles of quality manhood in your own life.

Manhood Statement
"As I help other brothers become better men, they help me as well!"

"He who guards his mouth keeps his life, but he who opens wide his lips comes to ruin."
~ Proverbs 13:3 AMP

* * *

"We have two ears and one mouth so that we can listen twice as much as we speak."
~ Epictetus

#100
Guard Your Words

The term, "*Spontaneous Trait Transference*" refers to the "*phenomenon where people are viewed to possess a trait or characteristic that they describe in someone else.*" So, if you tell someone that your boss is a selfish jerk, that person will subconsciously view you as a selfish jerk. However, if you describe someone else as a great and funny person, you'll be viewed as a great and funny person, without any logical basis or reason other than what you've said.

A quality male will only speak words about others, that he wants spoken about himself. So, guard the words you say about others and about yourself and make sure they're always beneficial and up-lifting. Of all the words that you'll hear spoken, you'll believe your own words the most; so, make them count.

Manhood Statement
"I guard the words I say about others and myself to make sure they're beneficial!"

"Keep and guard your heart with all vigilance and above all that you guard, for out of it flow the springs of life."
~ Proverbs 4:23 AMP

* * *

"True manhood isn't easy; adult boys need not apply."
~ Eric M. Watterson

#101
Guard Your Decision

The people around us have the ability to influence our lives by what they say and do to either encourage or discourage us. As you develop into a better man, there may be other males around you developing into more destructive and selfish males. You're bound to hear words, ideas, statements and beliefs that are contrary to your goal. So, make sure to guard your decision from any distracting concepts, situations or people.

There are negative ideas and concepts that will deter you in your pursuit of manhood; that is, if you let them. If you really desire to become a man of honor and love, should you really listen to people, opinions and songs that call women negative names or that encourage you to live in destructive, selfish and lustful ways? As a quality man, guard your decision to become better at all costs.

Manhood Statement
"I guard my decision from anything that'll hinder me from becoming a better man!"

"The path of those who live right is like the early morning light. It gets brighter and brighter until the full light of day."
~ Proverbs 4:18 ERV

* * *

"What we truly and earnestly aspire to be, that in some sense, we are. The mere aspiration, by changing the frame of the mind, for the moment realizes itself."
~ Anna Jameson

CLOSING
TOGETHER

"Make It Work Together"

together [tuh-geth -er] adverb - into or in one gathering, company, mass, place, or body: into or in union, proximity, contact, or collision, as two or more things: into or in relationship, association, business, or agreement, etc., as two or more persons: taken or considered collectively or conjointly:

No matter what you may have heard, think or believe about quality manhood, it'll only become a reality when you apply the work and effort needed to possess it. Ignorance is no excuse; don't let it stop you from your goal of becoming a better man.

The 101 principles of quality manhood listed here are meant to be a foundation towards helping you develop as a better man. They'll guide each male differently, so no matter what the ultimate destiny is for your life, take your own journey of quality manhood seriously. Do all you can to position yourself for consistent growth and learning.

Our boys need quality men to look up too. Our teenagers need patient men who'll help them find their way. Our immature adult males need strong men to correct them. Our women deserve compassionate men that'll care for them. Our children need caring men as fathers to protect them. Our families need committed men to lead them. Our society needs the unity and support of good men to help shape it. Our world needs the leadership of selfless men to advance it.

No matter what you are today, or what you're meant to be tomorrow, I pray that you join me, and all the other men of love, honor and character all over the world in being the very best examples of quality manhood that this world has ever seen.

I announce that, "Your manhood is valuable and needs to be seen. Your wife needs your manhood to be seen. Your children need your manhood to be seen. Your family needs your manhood to be seen. The entire world needs your manhood to be seen." Take a stand and let your manhood be seen!

Thanks for reading and God Bless You!

BIBLIOGRAPHY

References Used:

- The Bible: King James (KJV), Easy Read Version (ERV), God's Word (GW) and the Amplified (AMP) Versions

- Good Reads (http://goodreads.com)

- The Quotations Page (http://quotationspage.com)

- Dictionary.com (http://dictionary.reference.com)

"After removing him, God made David their king. This is what God said about him: 'I have found that David son of Jesse is the kind of man I like, a man who will do all I want him to do.'"
~ Acts 13:22 GNT

* * *

"Let the quality man you've been created to become out; the world is world complete without him."
~ Eric M. Watterson

OTHER BOOKS

Below are a few books by Eric M. Watterson. You may find them listed on Amazon.com or by clicking the title. You may also find these titles and others listed online at: CENTRY.me under "CENTRY Curriculum". Thank You!

- **Manhood 101: 101 Principles for Becoming a Better Man**
- **The Power of Touch: Your 14 Days Guide To A Stronger Relationship**
- **The Honor of Her: The Benefit of Honoring Her in Life & Relationship**
- **How Not 2 Hate Your Job: 13 Viewpoints for Satisfaction at Work**
- **How to Get Along with Everyone: Simple Keys for Success with Others**
- **Selfish or Selfless: Which One Are You?**
- **The Path of Forgiveness: How to Give & Receive Total Forgiveness**

- I Forgive You: Why You Should Always Forgive
- I Just Can't! How to Forgive the Unforgiveable
- Didn't You Forgive Me? How to Be Restored After Being Forgiven
- Your Strength As A Man
- DAD: Forgiving What He Was, Becoming What He Was Not
- **Constructive THOUGHTS, Workbook**
- **Productive WORDS, Workbook**
- **Excellent DECISIONS, Workbook**
- **Beneficial HABITS, Workbook**
- **Legendary CHARACTER, Workbook**
- **Awesome RELATIONSHIPS, Workbook**
- **Pursuing PURPOSE, Workbook**

FOLLOW US

Facebook.com/iamcentry

Twitter.com/iamcentry

Instagram.com/iamcentry/

YouTube Channel "iamCENTRY"

101 Principles for Becoming a Better Man

MORE INFORMATION

SERVE · HONOR · PROTECT

For more information concerning the CENTRY™ Brand, along with Additional Books, Courses, Mentoring, Services and Offers intended to Serve, Honor & Protect our wives, children, families, communities and the world, visit us online at:

"<u>CENTRY.me</u>" and "<u>CENTRYLeague.com</u>"

The CENTRY™ League "**Choose Greatness Personal Development & Mentoring Program**" consists of our series of workbooks and online courses that we use to mentor and coach males in 7 Specific Areas that will inspire, assist and lead them to Choose Greatness in their lives.

For more information visit:
<u>ChooseGreatness.me</u>

Made in the USA
Monee, IL
26 August 2022

12604133R00144